HALF DEAF,
COMPLETELY MAD

HALF DEAF, COMPLETELY MAD

The Chaotic Genius of Australia's Most Legendary Producer

TONY COHEN

with JOHN OLSON

Published by Black Inc., an imprint of Schwartz Books Pty Ltd
22–24 Northumberland Street
Collingwood VIC 3066, Australia
enquiries@blackincbooks.com
www.blackincbooks.com

9781760644536 (paperback)
9781743823088 (ebook)

A catalogue record for this
book is available from the
National Library of Australia

Cover design by Alex Ross
Text design and typesetting by Tristan Main
Cover image: Claudia Carey, courtesy of Billy Miller
Inside cover images and artwork: Peter Milne, *TV Week*, courtesy of the Cohen family

Every effort has been made to secure permissions for all images reproduced in
this volume. Please contact the publisher directly for further information.

... and the ant, five years laters, crept into the hole and Squatter was gone.

—Derek & Clive

Prologue

(1988)

'I need more!'

Okay.

'No, more!'

I gave him some more.

'You fucking idiot, Cohen. I can't hear myself.'

We were at Power Plant Recordings in Carlton, March 1988. I had been working on 'The Mercy Seat' for over six months. West Berlin, London, now back in Melbourne. Six different studios by my count, stumbling from one to the other. We'd gone quite mad.

Nick's headphones squealed with feedback.

'If that happens again I'll punch you in the face,' he warned. 'Turn my voice up.'

I put it on full blast and blew his head off.

Boof! He marched into the control room and punched me square on the nose. Fair enough, though he was being a cunt. I have no doubt 'The Mercy Seat' took a few years off my life. Recording was always an event, but when you got involved with Nick Cave and his mob you knew you were in for something serious. I was immersed. Crazed. It didn't help we were nearing the end of a nasty binge. Days without sleep, hallucinations. Everything was intense. Still, there was work to be done – Mick Harvey would see to that.

T.C.

'The Mercy Seat' was an incredibly hard recording to control. Forty-eight tracks, two tape machines locked together in sync. So many overdubs and still we needed more! Well, according to the artistes. I turned everything up and it was just noise. Chaos. The band hadn't performed the song live, instead building the track around a tape loop made at Hansa Tonstudio in West Berlin the year before. I love cutting tape and bouncing tracks. They're almost lost arts. Put on a show! Oh the fun of it, swinging the razor blade like a drunken sailor. The rhythm of the song became a loop of Mick Harvey's bass guitar, laid flat as he hit the strings with drumsticks. A click track, and a pretty bent one too.

LISTEN
'The Mercy Seat'—Nick Cave and the Bad Seeds

It took Nick a while to be happy with his vocals. Boy could he give you a hard time, with the microphone halfway down his throat. But that's the sound he wanted. Compressors couldn't cope with it so I'd often use more than one. Something fast and powerful to grab the peaks and another with valves to smooth it out. I had trouble balancing the spoken verses and sung chorus, but what do you sacrifice? The sound or the performance? Sometimes it's best to ignore a few mistakes. Music's not meant to be perfect, nothing is. I've got my dad's jazz records to thank for that insight. You can hit the odd fucking foul note as long as you give a fantastic performance.

It's about creating something that moves you.

T.C.

'The Mercy Seat' wore us down, but the best songs often do. We first mixed the track in January at The Kinks' Konk Studios in London, second at Strongroom, third at … I can't remember, but each effort was a step closer to making it work. Practise. Sometimes it might be better to hand a recording over to someone with fresh ears to pick up on things you've missed, but we had Mick. He was always the voice of reason, the relatively sober one. Which I guess helped! I loved working with him. We would talk as we went, bringing instruments in and out. Wrestling with the noise. Mixing had become a good collaboration and lots of fun. The final pass was done live and I was extremely happy with the result.

The album *Tender Prey* was now complete.

'Watching Alice' had been mixed earlier by Chris Thompson at The Studio, formerly known as Richmond Recorders. It seems I'd gone missing for a while. There's always a first! Maybe I was booked for another project. Or hiding under the bed? All very possible. Chris would help out if I went missing. We were old friends and didn't need to talk about anything – he knew what to do. I'd spent enough time in the studio anyway. The mixes were sent off and part payment withheld due to excessive distortion.

T.C.

By the time 'The Mercy Seat' was released as a single I was back in London. But something was rotten. What was fun in the early days had turned ugly. I was burning out. Before the second show of a short tour I was done as the Bad Seeds live engineer. I made it to the door, but didn't want to go in. We finished mixing the readings for Nick's debut novel, *And the Ass Saw the Angel*, at 7 a.m. on Monday, 1 August, and that was it. Already half my life had been spent in a recording studio. It was time to get out of the business for a while.

I was thirty-one years old.

Tony Cohen 'T.C.'

(1957)

My grandfather was appalled by me as a teenager. I had hair down to my knees and listened to The Beatles and The Rolling Stones. He'd been in the Middle East on horseback with a rifle and bayonet chopping Turks' heads off. I've got photos around the caravan of him sitting on a camel, with the pyramids in the background. He was a soldier in World War I, a member of the Light Horse Brigade in Egypt.

He lied about his age to get there.

The war was a big influence on his life. It wrecked him, and he would never speak of it. Instead, he would have a drink. Who knew then about post-traumatic stress disorder and its effects? I'm sure he had it, he must have. They'd all thought the war would be such a great adventure. I remember asking him what he thought of the atom bomb. He said to blow up civilians, women and children was criminal, even though it saved so many lives.

T.C.

My name is Anthony Lawrence Cohen. I was born at 9 a.m. on Tuesday, 4 June 1957 at the Jessie McPherson Community Hospital to parents Margaret and Phillip. I'm Melbourne born and bred, and proud of it.

The Mackinoltys, my mother's side of the family, came to Australia very early in the piece. There was something dodgy going on, Irish convicts I believe. Not a great deal is known. I should look into it at some stage, but it was probably nothing more than stealing a loaf of bread. My great-aunt, however, wouldn't have a bar of it. 'There is no way!' she would say, which only made us more convinced it was true. My father's family arrived more recently, pre–World War II. His parents were non-practising Jews, refugees from Manchester, England, who came to Australia for a better life.

Dad took many jobs and started off at Myer department store as a window dresser of all things. He ended up on the road as a travelling shoe salesman visiting country stores. I think he enjoyed it.

T.C.

We moved from East Ringwood to a three-bedroom weatherboard in the bayside suburb of Mentone. It was the middle of 1964 and my younger brother, Martin, was three. I went to St Patrick's Primary School.

Tony at St Patrick's Primary School, 1960s. Image courtesy of the Cohen family.

Mentone was a quiet 1960s middle-class suburb. I've been told I spent a lot of time sitting in front of the television. *Dr Who*, *Lost in Space*, *Thunderbirds* and a bit of food every now and then kept me occupied. Mum would be in the kitchen battling away like so many women of that era. Cooking, baking cakes. She always had the radio on and by then stations were playing pop music.

The Beatles had just toured Australia.

It's only in recent years I've come to appreciate the beauty of those early songs I heard on the radio. I became interested in The Beatles in their later psychedelic period, with *Sgt. Pepper's Lonely Hearts Club Band*. In fact, that was my first record, and *Gather Me* by Melanie Safka, the album with 'Brand New Key' on it, a song about rollerskates. I'm proud *Sgt. Pepper's* was my first album, I was off to a good start! I've still got it. The cover is in good condition, complete with the original inserts and I never cut out the moustaches. Of course the record itself is now unplayable.

T.C.

In Grade Five I started at St Bede's, a Catholic boys' college in Mentone. I don't have great memories of that time. I was reasonably good at art, English and history. But mathematics and science? I was quite bad, and I hated sport.

Christian Brothers always had you dressed in a football uniform. It was the worst. I was a skinny pale kid, so would find a spot on the ground the furthest point away from the action. I remember standing around kicking the ground, minding my own business, when suddenly the ball landed at my feet. I looked up and saw eighteen much bigger blokes coming straight at me. I looked at the ball. I wasn't going to pick it up, no way. What am I, stupid? These guys were going to jump all over me. Instead I pivoted, hurdled the fence and ran home, a good fifteen minutes away. I can still hear the teacher yelling, 'Cohen, get back, you're supposed to pick up the ball!'

Not everybody wants to do the same thing in life.

I should have been a good student, but it depends on your teachers too. St Bede's was strict, and some of the Brothers were like Nazis. It was difficult to learn when they were barking at you all the time. Mum would write notes for me to get out of football. She had compassion and realised it wasn't for me. It worked out well because I got put into golf. I would turn up at the course and get a card, fill in a fake score, then go and smoke bongs with my mates. I was starting to get into pot. It was much better than standing in front of footballs. Unfortunately, a nasty maths teacher turned up at the golf course one day for a spot check. Not knowing what clubs to use I had a 1-wood on the putting green, so my cover was blown.

T.C.

Choir was a bludge that got you out of things you didn't want to do, like schoolwork. I found it interesting. Perhaps it showed that even early in the piece I had an aptitude for music? In a vague sort of way. Very vague.

The choirmaster was Brother Leopold, one of the better teachers at the school. He had the most perfect oval-shaped head of any person I have seen. All the kids called him Egghead. He would exaggerate every movement of his mouth when singing, which had us in hysterics. I didn't like the songs very much so I would mime. That was too easy. As long as you opened your mouth and looked the part, he didn't know. Eventually the old bastard started walking up and down with his ear in front of everyone's mouth, likely to find out who was singing out of tune, but maybe he was onto us? You couldn't get away with miming when he started that.

T.C.

'FOUR FLOORS OF FOOTSIE FASHION!'

Mister Figgins was a shoe store at 163 Swanston Street in the city. It was a huge building, in the days when department stores were en vogue. My dad was the manager.

Owner Don Figgins was a trendy dude in his twenties with long hair and tight flares. He was a clever marketer and his face was on all the advertising, a black-and-white silhouette. He even had stickers: 'MISTER FIGGINS HAS ARRIVED'. I went up on the roof, peeled the backs off and dropped them in the wind. It was hysterical. One stuck to a car window and another a passing umbrella. Ah, the things that amuse young minds.

Swanston Street was for young people. Looking into the store from the footpath was a narrow window at eye level. Behind it models would walk back and forth, so all you could see was their feet, wearing the dreadful platform shoes people bought in those days. Men's ones too, like the band KISS would soon wear. The basement was full of them. I'd hang around on weekends and over the summer school holidays and got to hear a lot of new music.

I took John Lennon very seriously. His records, apart from one or two duds, made you think. *Plastic Ono Band*, his first solo album, was released in December 1970. One of the staff had just bought a copy and wanted to play it in the store, so he instructed me to skip track four, 'Working Class Hero', to censor the word 'fuck' in its lyrics. No worries! The album played all day and of course I often forgot.

'A working class hero is something to be.'

T.C.

'The sky is not just a blue line at the top of the page.'

'What?' I replied.

'It extends all the way to the horizon.'

It's funny what you remember. I was drawing with my next-door neighbour Peter Hatwell and got upset with him for criticising me, but he was right. An image has depth.

Peter was a music fanatic. He was a few years older than me and went to the Anglican boys' school Mentone Grammar. They had their own Army Cadet Unit, which Peter hated. He wanted to be a surfie and I'd get him ugg boots from Figgins to sell to his mates. At the end of 1971 I moved to Cheltenham and we lost touch. I was thirteen, with all of the ratbag behaviour that comes with that age. I'd been given a small stereo reel-to-reel tape recorder with a 'Sound-On-Sound' button, which meant you could record sounds on top of each other.

I started getting really curious.

Ian Dickson, Barry Dick and John Ahern were friends in a garage band. All their gear was set up in my parents' lounge room with my tape recorder and a few plastic microphones. One practice the drummer didn't show, so I sat down and had a bash. I found I could keep time! Not very well, but the guitarist couldn't tune up so I was in good company. We played bad covers of The Rolling Stones and Creedence Clearwater Revival. Mum had a great suggestion for a band name, which was Boondoggle. It means incapable of doing anything correctly. Someone will use that one day and it will be very funny. Instead, we called ourselves Epitaph.

T.C.

My parents bought me an old broken-down Canora drum kit from the *Trading Post* newspaper. Dad drove out to the middle of nowhere to pick it up and my career as a drummer was off!

Drums are a difficult instrument to practise because the noise pisses people off. I can't imagine why? One day after school I was banging on my kit in the garage when I heard some drums coming from the house opposite. Enter my new friend Chris Thompson. He was a kindred spirit. Chris was as bad at drumming as me, and shared a similar passion for music. We soon spent every night after school in his small bedroom out the back, smoking and misbehaving. Chris had homemade speakers and we'd sit around them listening to music very closely. It was enthralling.

As our circle of friends increased, Chris's bedroom became a bit cramped. My grandfather was not too well at the time, so Mum and Dad built a granny flat, which gobbled up my bedroom. They put walls up in the garage and turned it into a place for me to live. It was great – black, with purple carpet. Not everyone's cup of tea! We killed a lot of hours and brain cells in that room, if I remember correctly.

T.C.

My brother, Martin, didn't hang around with us and had his own friends. We couldn't relate well to each other. He was more of a sports person, never a huge music fan, and had different tastes to mine.

If I love something I go apeshit over it. The Beatles, The Rolling Stones, Creedence Clearwater Revival, Black Sabbath, Jethro Tull, Pink Floyd, Stevie Wonder. I had my era of music and if my friends didn't know about an album I'd make damn sure they did, I've always been very pushy like that.

I'm a fan of listening to albums, and in full.

That's what the artist intended – a collection of songs, in a particular order. Even if there's one or two you don't like, it's an entire package. To pick out individual songs seems like a silly thing to do. Imagine The Beatles' *White Album* without 'Revolution 9'? As a kid I thought that song was rubbish, then came to love it, with stories of Paul McCartney dying in a car crash, fire noises and screaming. When I hear it now I'm immediately transported back to my parents' garage at four o'clock in the morning. It's the same for Creedence's 'I Heard It Through the Grapevine'.

T.C.

Dad is a devout Christian. He converted to Catholicism to marry my mother. They go to church every week and love it. Unfortunately, or fortunately, it never quite took with me.

Godspell and *Jesus Christ Superstar* appeared in the early 1970s. The Australian production of *Jesus Christ Superstar* featured The Ferrets' Billy Miller and K.D. Firth, but I'll get to them later. The musicals were very popular with young people, so the parish priest decided to put on a 'rock mass' and Epitaph was chosen as the band. It was good fun, the usual Sunday morning service but with a bit of singing from *Godspell*.

'Prepare ye underpants for the Lord.'

A shriek went right through the church when the drums came in. It was a big fill, which I hit rather hard because I was nervous. The old ladies hit the roof! Mum and Dad sat extremely proud, if a bit embarrassed that I'd caused three or four heart attacks among the congregation.

Oh well, it was the priest's fault. He should have advertised it as a young people's service. I spent the rest of my church years outside smoking cigarettes and running around local school halls recording garage bands with my tape recorder. I loved it.

T.C.

Most drummers set a beat and the band play to it. The Rolling Stones' drummer, Charlie Watts, plays to Keith Richards' guitar, so is slightly behind. It gives the band a totally unique sound and served them for many years.

I saw The Rolling Stones perform at Kooyong Tennis Stadium on Sunday, 18 February 1973. It was a life-changing experience. I'd queued up with my mates overnight in sleeping bags to get tickets. Of course, we ended up in the middle of the stadium – corporate dudes get the best seats. *Exile on Main St* was the band's latest album and Mick Jagger was strutting about the stage at his absolute peak, with Keith, Charlie and Bill joined by legendary sidemen Nicky Hopkins, Bobby Keys and Jim Price. What an education!

The band had big African American bodyguards throwing rose petals into the audience. It sounds odd now, but non-Europeans were a new sight. It was the dying days of the White Australia policy and Melbourne wasn't anything like the multicultural city it is today. This different world suited me just fine. A girl was sitting up on her boyfriend's shoulders with her top off. The police came to drag her away, but Jagger noticed and threatened to stop the show. The coppers looked around and saw a few thousand fairly pent-up young people, so they left her alone.

I didn't realise at the time, but I'd just seen one of the greatest acts in the world. The musicianship and songs, fuck. *Sticky Fingers*, I wish I'd recorded that album.

T.C.

Dad's jazz mad. Some of the music he exposed me to was really exciting. Unfortunately, he also loves musical theatre, which I loathe. Fred Astaire, Ginger Rogers and all that sort of stuff.

He took me to a Benny Goodman show at Festival Hall in March. What a gas. I'd never seen so many bald heads in my life! Goodman had the great Lionel Hampton playing the vibraphone. It was beautiful, his grunting was so loud you could hear it over the top of the band. 'UGH! UGH! UGH!' Punk rock? Forget Sid Vicious and those jokers. These old boys had it long before.

More Arse than Class

(1973)

A guy quite a bit older than me had a band that played each weekend at the Croydon Hotel. The gigs erupted into a huge brawl on a regular basis. It was fascinating, and I would hang around to watch.

I was getting into acid and things were starting to look dishonest. I'd go to school and see the Brothers in a completely different light. They didn't seem to practise what they preached. Some enjoyed discipline more than they should, and I could see it in their eyes. And the teachings ... This bloke what? He got killed and came back again? The virgin what? Virgin birth? No, hang on. I'm having a bit of trouble with this.

T.C.

In May, a friend and I were caught smoking something we shouldn't. We were right out of luck when the Brothers came searching for stolen books and found hash in my locker. And a few heart pills which spun you out.

We were hauled into the principal's office.

Brother Peter sat staring at us for what felt like an hour. Suddenly he went bright red in the face, with big bug-eyes and throbbing veins. 'SATAN HAS POSSESSED YOUR SOULS!' he yelled. It was like an exorcism. I freaked out – we'd been expelled.

Getting kicked out of school at age fifteen was considered pretty poor form, but it was the best thing St Bede's did for me. It was the start of first-term holidays. Mum and Dad knew something wasn't right when I came home with a bag full of my belongings! I'm sure they could have begged the principal to take me back, but they could see I hated school and wasn't heading in any academic direction. It was going to be music, somehow.

Lawrence Costin was the Saturday afternoon sports announcer for Melbourne radio station 3DB. He was best man at Mum and Dad's wedding and Lawrence is my middle name. Due to an alignment of the planets, he knew Bill Armstrong, owner of the legendary Armstrong Studios, and organised an interview for me. That's how this all started.

What a lucky lad.

T.C.

In Sydney there was Albert Studios and EMI, but in Melbourne it was Armstrong Studios. It's a huge part of Australian music history and was responsible for some of the greatest recordings ever.

Armstrong Studios, 1972. Image courtesy of Bill Armstrong.

Armstrong's was located at 180 Bank Street, South Melbourne. It was a big four-storey building with five studios in the basement. There were two 16-track studios for music and three 4-track studios for jingles and voice overs. Studio 1 was huge, big enough to fit a seventy-piece orchestra. Studio 2 was a smaller rock 'n' roll room, much like the layout of Abbey Road Studios in London. Every other floor of the building was completely empty, except for Bill's office at the top – right in the corner.

I was terrified.

On Bill's desk sat a Pyrox wire recorder as an ornament. I lied and said I was sixteen and on school holidays, and to my surprise he replied, 'Alright, two weeks' work experience and we'll see how you go.' I was the studio odd-job boy, which means to do anything you're told. No worries! I worked like a maniac, delivering tapes, making coffee, getting the lunches. Foul jobs, too, like cleaning the toilets. After my two weeks were done, I turned up expecting to be sent packing but no one said a word. So I just kept coming back.

My first week's pay was $17 – I was so young I spent it on lollies. And hash.

T.C

Early Rolling Stones records are quite boring, they're just copies of American blues music. But slowly the band got on track. Their first single, 'Come On', was recorded at Olympic Studios in London in 1963 by Roger Savage.

He is one of the greats.

Roger was a migrant to Australia, a 'Ten Pound Pom', and brought with him the latest recording knowledge from England. I couldn't help but soak it up. Armstrong's trained people on the job, so you learnt by doing it. There was no such thing as audio schools, no one really knew this job existed. It was the other side of the glass, where all people did was fiddle a few knobs. A little naive, I know. Sound recording is an art created by talented engineers, not just musicians, and I learnt from the best: Roger Savage, Ernie Rose, Graham Owens, Ian MacKenzie and Ross Cockle. They were brilliant.

Roger monitored loud. I was told he was deaf in one ear, though I don't know if that's true. The story was someone left an oscillator on at Olympic Studios and Roger came in the next morning, switched on the power and a test tone blasted flat chat out the speakers, perforating his eardrum. I did notice he would often turn his head to one side to listen, so perhaps that was his good ear? Or maybe it was his bad ear and he didn't like what he was hearing!

I can see Roger now at the mixing desk with a cigarette in his mouth, squinting through smoke as it burnt his eyes. He always looked into the studio and by watching the musicians, rather than fiddling with knobs and dials, he knew exactly what to do. It was spectacular. His hands would instinctively glide across the desk.

T.C.

Armstrong Studios started in 1965 in a terrace house at 100 Albert Road, South Melbourne. That's where Roger and another great, John Sayers, recorded classics like John Farnham's 'Sadie (The Cleaning Lady)', Russell Morris's 'The Real Thing', The Masters Apprentices' 'Turn Up Your Radio' and Daddy Cool's 'Eagle Rock'.

The new Bank Street studio opened in December 1972.

When I arrived, construction wasn't yet complete. Studio 1 looked like a dark cave, with wires hanging and exposed cables where walls had yet to go in. When it rained heavily it would flood. But things started to come together – Ernie Rose in particular worked like a slave. He liked to get his hands dirty and helped build the studio from the ground up. I'd be there stapling sheets of fibreglass to panels of chipboard and getting glass shards in my skin that 100 showers couldn't get out.

Ernie had been a truck driver, I believe, before Bill provided him with the opportunity to be an engineer. I'm sure many people have a natural aptitude for the job but don't know it, especially in my day. Construction? I wasn't a natural at that.

T.C.

The first session I recall working on is Billy Thorpe and the Aztecs' *More Arse than Class*. It's a well-known album, mostly due to a gatefold cover featuring the band's arses. It was recorded in Studio 2 with Ian MacKenzie toward the end of 1973. I would often work with Ian, and he was very generous with his knowledge.

Billy Thorpe and the Aztecs were Billy Thorpe, Warren Morgan, Gil Matthews and Teddy Toi. They were royalty. Fair dinkum Oz rock 'n' roll. I ran errands for the band and was terrified of Billy. Some people you are in awe of turn out to be complete monsters!

'Where is that little cunt?' I knew that meant me.

'Here, Mr Thorpe,' I chirped.

'Good. Go get me some beer.'

Everybody at Armstrong's went to the same pub, the Town Hall Hotel. It was opposite the studio at 137 Bank Street. But I was sixteen and the pub staff knew exactly who I was.

'Sorry, Mr Thorpe,' I mumbled. 'I'm not old enough.'

'Fuck that, I'll write you a note.'

He did and they sold me the beer. I was in a different world.

T.C.

Billy had a wall of Marshall amplifiers that were so loud the studio window would bend in and out. He'd come into the control room and complain that the sound going to tape wasn't as big as what he was hearing from his amps. The microphone diaphragm couldn't handle the volume, so the sound was tiny. Even with my limited knowledge I guessed that.

LISTEN
'Slowly Learning How'—Billy Thorpe and the Aztecs

I'd go home for the weekend, come back on Monday morning and the band was still at it. There'd be members passed out under layers of fish-and-chip paper, hamburger wrappers and empty longnecks of Melbourne Bitter. I didn't understand. How could these guys work for three days nonstop? I didn't know it was drugs, I had no idea what speed was. I just thought they were a dedicated bunch. I was learning the art of sound recording – in a very roundabout way.

T.C.

From odd jobs I got promoted to mono dubbing boy. It was awful. Primarily it consisted of making copies of advertising jingles. Hundreds and hundreds of them on 5-inch tape spools and cartridges for radio stations. The general public would also bring in jobs, wedding recordings they'd want transferred or a cassette to be fixed. They were interesting skills to learn, but it was tedious work.

On weekends Epitaph would record in Studio 2. Armstrong's was great like that, they considered it training. A bit of studio time and tape was worth the investment. I had no idea what I was doing so the recordings were rough. It would take me eight hours to get one microphone to work! I'd patch things in, hit record, then run out and play the drums. I mixed everything over and over again, trying to figure out why it sounded so bad. I was too green to realise that crappy musicians playing covers is never going to end well.

Don't work with amateurs!

Finally, Roger called me to his office and asked where I wanted to go. I was given a choice: stereo dubbing or mono dubbing. Stereo would lead to recording music, while mono meant advertising. Too easy – I had no intention of working in advertising. Some people did, it was good money, but I just wanted to record music. So I got the big promotion.

The Boy from the Stars

(1974)

Armstrong's stereo dubbing room will always hold a special place in my heart. It was square-shaped, with shiny red walls and carpet, soft couches and huge Tannoy speakers. I would sit and make cassette listening copies of the latest albums from quarter-inch tapes.

My fondest memories were assisting engineers on their sessions. I'd run around with microphones and do whatever they told me. Everyone wanted Roger for orchestra recordings and I had the pleasure of assisting him on the album *Linda* for the middle-of-the-road genre singer Linda George. The producer was a big-time Canadian, Jack Richardson, who had recorded Alice Cooper. It was the first time I saw Americans at work.

LISTEN
'Mama's Little Girl'—Linda George

I was appalled! Americans carry on with so much bullshit. 'Woohoo, Yeehaw, Kickass' and all that. I guess it's just the way they talk. 'Let's get this turkey in the shops!' Jack would say, which sounded a bit rude. What on earth was he talking about? I thought he was saying the album was shit, but he was suggesting we move the session along. Some expressions don't translate.

T.C.

The first 16-track recorder in Australia appeared at Armstrong's in 1971 and was very popular. The machines kept breaking down, but the sound was great. You could slam the meters into the red.

Graham Thirkell and Bill Armstrong with the Optro tape machine, 1971.
Image courtesy of Bill Armstrong.

Armstrong's had their own brand of tape machines called Optro, which were designed and built by local audio pioneer Graham Thirkell. He was the founder of the company Optronics. Graham's ideas were revolutionary, but he never quite got what he wanted, so in the early days there were a lot of problems. Optro machines had big modules underneath called track amps, the guts of each track, with circuits that would now be the size of a match head. The modules made bad connections to the motherboard, so sometimes to get one of the bloody things to work you'd have to pull it out and slam it back in as hard as you could. It was a nuisance.

I remember Graham Owens recording an orchestra for a Marlboro cigarette commercial. There was much slamming of modules that day! The tracks on the tape machine packed it in and Graham ended up with only four working. Poor bastard, he was having a nervous breakdown.

T.C.

Graham Thirkell never had enough funding to manufacture his equipment. I once went to the Optronics factory in Huntingdale and there were ladies with handkerchief hair scarves soldering circuit boards. I don't know what their qualifications were. Graham would then cover these boards in epoxy – blobs of sealed plastic to hide his secret designs. It meant that when something went wrong you couldn't fix one component. Instead, you'd have to take the whole board out and replace it with another.

The stereo dubbing room had several quarter-inch Optro 2-track machines. If one didn't work I was told to leave it outside the workshop with a note for the technicians. That didn't end well when every machine broke down. I had eight of them lined up along the corridor with a sign on each: 'RUNS BACKWARDS', 'WON'T RECORD', 'WON'T DO ANYTHING'. Roger Savage happened to be showing a group of potential Japanese investors the Optro equipment that day!

Oh dear, what a fuck-up.

All these dudes in suits walked right past. It was most amusing, but not for Roger. He probably wanted to tear my head off, though what could he do? I knew nothing about it. I was just doing what I was told and it happened to be the wrong day to do it.

T.C.

Armstrong's was sold to David Syme & Co and became Armstrong Audio Video (AAV) in March 1974. Bill made a huge profit. He was probably glad to be done with the pressure of running the business, but stayed on as managing director.

Everything changed.

David Syme were owners of *The Age* newspaper in Melbourne and had big plans. Empty floors at Bank Street were filled with telecine machines, videotape and state-of-the-art editing for television studios to outsource promos and advertisements. The official opening was in June. Overseas acts came in and the studio developed an excellent reputation.

Some couldn't believe we had a facility like it in Australia. Cat Stevens recorded the single 'Another Saturday Night' while on tour that month and I was the tape operator, though it wasn't one of my finest hours.

LISTEN
'Another Saturday Night' — Cat Stevens

'Another Saturday Night' was recorded by Ernie Rose in Studio 1. Ernie created the slickest-sounding recordings. He was so good with a tape machine – an artist, I would say. It was my job on the session to rewind the tape and hit record when told. I was Ernie's remote control. Cat Stevens had a big band, musicians of the highest calibre, with guys playing congas and the like. I was so amazed that I forgot to rewind the tape ready for the next take! It made Ernie look slack so I was thrown out, and rightly so. You have to follow every moment of a recording session. 'Get someone else in,' Ernie demanded. I learnt a lot by getting sacked. It made me cross and I wanted to prove myself.

T.C.

Shortly after I stuck my ugly beak in, the Optro 24-track arrived and the 16-track machines were moved to the smaller studios. At the time, I was saving like mad and bought myself a Teac A-3340 4-track quarter-inch tape recorder.

I spent hours experimenting, making recordings with school friends I was still in touch with. With 4-tracks you could record four different people, or three and mix it down onto a spare track and then overdub more. We made hysterical recordings of our school experiences, imitating the Brothers and their services. I'd also take my 4-track to gigs, recording garage bands that were playing around local halls. That's how I learnt the basics. I got some really good recordings, even of my own band, Epitaph, which was still struggling along.

T.C.

We would make guitar amps from circuits printed in the *Electronics Australia* magazine. They blew up regularly, but you could get replacement components from Radio Parts. At the checkout, our tray would contain three or four items and our pockets thirty or forty.

Being a drummer was hard work. The guitarists had amps, the singer a column PA, but I had to bash as hard as possible. I'd bang nails into the stage to keep the drums from falling over the edge. We would play for a long time, two or three hours, but only knew ten songs, so would play 12-bar blues to make up the time. It would go on and on, with me belting desperately under the stage spotlights. At one gig the singer's girlfriend made us satin shirts to wear. The material didn't breathe so they were ridiculously hot. During one extended 12-bar blues the drums suddenly stopped. The band looked around to see I'd fallen off my stool and passed out. Very dignified!

Epitaph demo tape, 1974. Image courtesy of the Cohen family.

The highlight of Epitaph's career was supporting Skyhooks at a school dance, long before anyone had heard of them. The 'hooks had make-up and smoke bombs but most of the audience came to see us, then left after our crappy effort. Years later I spoke to Skyhooks' guitarist Red Symons about it, but he didn't remember the gig.

T.C.

Opposite the railway station was the Chelsea Dance Hall. The building is still there. On a Saturday night you could see bands like Billy Thorpe and the Aztecs and AC/DC. I didn't realise what a privilege that was at the time.

We would drive to shows at Ormond Hall in Prahran, called the Reefer Cabaret, which later became known as Stoned Again. The cops would walk in and all the drug dealers would disappear out the exits! I saw Split Enz there and it was wild. They looked so strange with their weird hairdos and asymmetrical clothes that I didn't know if what I was seeing was really happening. Maybe it was the acid I'd taken? When I saw them later on television I realised it was the band, as well as the drugs.

I saw Ayers Rock play at the Reefer Cabaret and was mesmerised. Graham Owens had just recorded the band's album *Big Red Rock* at AAV. Ayers Rock were experienced musicians at the peak of their powers and bass player Duncan McGuire, who I ended up spending a lot of time with, and drummer Mark Kennedy were amazing. When I saw Mark play drums I gave up because I could never be that good. I think I made the right choice.

T.C.

The Boy from the Stars was recorded in Studio 1 in September. It was Jim Keays' first album since leaving The Masters Apprentices so EMI put a lot of faith in the project. It was very ambitious, but I'm not sure they succeeded.

A hotshot producer came down from Sydney. I couldn't understand what he was trying to do, he wanted everything so over the top. Like Phil Spector. He threw everything at it, strings, choirs. Some of the best musicians in Melbourne got called in. The musical director for the project was Chain guitarist Phil Manning. 'Okay, gentlemen,' he'd say, 'let's tune up' and the first person at their instrument was drummer Mark Kennedy. I'd never seen anything like it, nor have I since. A huge drum kit and every tom was tuned to perfection. Add to that he could play the damn things.

Everything about the recording was big.

'Kid's Blues' was a rock song so they got thirteen guitarists for the session. No, twelve guitarists. Or was it ten? Whatever, it didn't matter because Lobby Loyde was one of them. His guitar was so loud the sound bled into every microphone in the studio, including the drums. They couldn't get rid of it! Phil Manning was tearing his hair out. Lobby's guitar was everywhere.

I engineered some of the album but was mostly the assistant, so spent many hours doing drop-ins and other jobs the main engineers didn't want to do. It was a strange experience.

T.C.

If recording *The Boy from the Stars* was bizarre, playing at Sunbury in January 1975 was even more so. Jim planned to launch the album at the festival and I was in charge of playing the sound effects.

It was a glorious disaster.

Jim was lowered onto the stage in a flying saucer for the opening track, 'The Boy from the Stars'. I had all of the effects on tape, the sound of ships landing and taking off, but his flying saucer didn't work. You can imagine. There was smoke everywhere, sound effects playing and the stupid thing wouldn't land. The film *This Is Spinal Tap* hadn't yet been made, but they got it so right.

LISTEN
'The Boy from the Stars'—Jim Keays

Jim was still halfway up in the air when the effects ran out. There was silence as I frantically rewound the tape. I don't think the audience was too impressed, but they probably forgot about it as everyone was just waiting for Thorpie to come on. Poor Jim. He was a lovely man, but *The Boy from the Stars* wasn't a well-thought-out project. I don't think I ever heard from the producer again, it might have done him in. He wasted half a million bucks.

One of the Mob

(1975)

I would work on projects other engineers wouldn't touch, like the late Stevie Dunstan's album *Magnetic Fields*. Stevie's great-grandfather was Abel Hoadley of Hoadley's Chocolates, inventors of the Violet Crumble and the Polly Waffle. He was heir to the fortune, and quite mad.

Stevie had played the 'Zapophone' on *The Boy from the Stars*. He was very clever and built his own synthesisers, all in clear plastic boxes full of flashing lights. The lights had nothing to do with the sound, it was just for the look. He would appear at the studio every couple of months. His flying saucer would land on the roof and the older engineers would run for the hills, leaving me to deal with him. Sucker! They didn't want to listen to his crazy electronic music. It was all blips, blops, squeaks and squawks. I thought it was pretty good, but what would I know? I don't have an ear for extreme electronic music.

Stevie had spent years on *Magnetic Fields*. He recorded most of the album himself, except for a couple of tracks on side one, which were recorded at Armstrong's before my time. 'Blue & Green' was the most memorable and actually sounds like a song. Side two was a bit hard to get your head around, it went berko.

Stevie was a man of few words.

'Tony, the balloons!' he would say. 'I want the balloons to go up, instead of down.'

I'd cut the tape, turn it around backwards and stick it back together so 'BLOOP-Bloop-bloop' became 'bloop-Bloop-BLOOP'. With that simple task done, he'd sit in the stereo dubbing room and listen to the album from start to finish in total darkness.

Strange Stevie. I suspect the edits were just an excuse for him to come to the studio and hear the album loud on the big Tannoy speakers. That's all he really wanted – to play his music.

T.C.

The stereo dubbing room was my territory. A lot of bizarre things would go on in there. Sex, drugs and very loud music. What a place for a young hippie to work!

Joe Cocker played the Sidney Myer Music Bowl on 25 February. He had a huge band who all turned up at AAV after the gig to listen to a demo tape. I was still lurking about at that late hour so they were sent to the stereo dubbing room. We put on the tape. It was some Australian singer, I can't remember who. Everyone was taking it very seriously so she must have had something, either that or one of the band members wanted to jump her bones. They skinned up a spliff and started laughing among themselves. The odour was weird, it smelled like shit. 'I'll have some of that,' I piped up. Everyone looked at me and watched. There was sniggering as I turned green, and laughing out loud as I bolted to the dunny for a huge yet pleasant chunder.

It was the strongest weed I'd ever had.

When I came in the next day the remnants were scattered on the floor. Greedily, I scooped it up. *This is going to blow my friends' minds*, I thought. But when we smoked it nothing happened, it was just weed. Years later I realised the band had spiked the spliff with opium, which was why I vomited. They introduced me to a lifetime of misery! Not quite, but it was a shock.

T.C.

I was promoted from tape operator to recording demos. It probably happened too soon, but I gained a lot of experience in a short space of time. I made mistakes and quickly learnt from them.

Studio 2 at AAV was my training ground. The mixing desk had an innovative new patchbay, one of Thirkell's ideas. Instead of running a cord to connect one piece of equipment to another, there were rows of small light bulbs. You would press a button on the top and a button on the side, then a light would appear and patch something through. As far as I know it never actually worked – we would use a normal patchbay instead – but it was an extremely entertaining distraction for musicians who were bored.

Many people tried to write F-U-C-K with the lights. It was a fun and challenging game. Remember, this was before we had *Space Invaders*. If you didn't hold a certain number of buttons down a light you depended on for part of a letter might switch off. One session there were five or six blokes huddled around, pressing buttons. They got to the end of the letter 'K' and the whole thing went up in smoke! So that was the end of Thirkell's patchbay. I wish I could remember who the band was.

I can't recall much about early recordings, except that they happened. Some were so disastrous I'd call off the session. One technique was to punch holes in a metal Kodak film canister and place a cut-up ping-pong ball inside. I'd stick it under the mixing desk, set fire to the ball, and as smoke emerged complain the desk was broken.

T.C.

I had many interesting jobs at AAV. In 1975 Bill Armstrong started 3EA, a government ethnic radio station which a few years later became SBS. I remember setting up some of that in Studio 3.

I was also the engineer for Bill on a session by jazz musician Smacka Fitzgibbon. It was done in an afternoon. That's how those dudes recorded – you'd mic them up, get a level and they'd play the song. I have no idea why Bill set me loose on the recording, perhaps he wanted to find out if I was any good? I mimicked the senior engineers and stuffed a pillow in the kick drum to dampen the sound. Smacka was horrified! 'Do you want to put cotton wool in my mouth too?' I felt like a dill, but I understood later what he was saying. It was completely the wrong sound for jazz.

There were quite a few forgettable sessions. The German opera singer I could have done without. He looked like a derro – a great big man dressed in overcoats on a hot day, carrying shopping bags. He would sit down and pull out jars of honey and lemon for his voice, then present me with a chewed-up cassette of piano accompaniment. The sound quality was appalling! I'd transfer it to multitrack and he'd sing along. He wasn't fussy about where he got the cassettes, but he was very fussy about his voice. Once I got cheeky and put a bit of reverb on. He came in the next day and was furious.

'This is not my voice!' he roared.

I was bamboozled, as was Roger Savage, who finally figured out it was the reverb that had this man so upset, so he gave him another free go at it.

T.C.

I was sent to record the great country-and-western artist Chad Morgan live at a strip club. I don't know how I got there because I wasn't even eighteen. It was quite an education, but I probably wasn't the best choice for the job.

I arrived with a 4-track tape recorder, mixer, microphones, leads and some headphones. The only space to set up was on a toilet seat backstage. It was in the change room for the strippers, so I saw a lot more than other young blokes at that age. 'Don't mind a bit of titty, do you, love?' Oh no, not all! Under the bright fluorescent lights backstage, the costumes the girls took off – feather boas, sequinned body stockings and things like that – had all seen better days. So, too, had some of the 'artists'. Girls mostly, I think. It was very tacky, but onstage in the dark, bathed in coloured lights, everything looked beautiful.

A drunk burst in, dressed in a long overcoat with a bottle of whisky in his pocket, and had a violent chunder in the next cubicle. I couldn't believe it – Chad Morgan! I started to think about packing up, when all of a sudden he was onstage.

LISTEN
'The Fatal Wedding' – Chad Morgan

I became an instant fan. Chad was completely out of it but got up and performed. I never thought that stuff happened until I saw it with my own eyes. Show business, eh? I'm told some of the recording appeared on *One of the Mob*, an album Ian MacKenzie was working on. It's a bit corny, but of its era.

T.C.

I turned eighteen in June. All my mates were still at school, and I was driving around in the studio delivery van. It was a red Mini with the Armstrong's logo on the side. I'd bought the car the year before and thought I was hot shit.

Ross Cockle had been promoted up the ladder when I started and was recording Little River Band's first album in Studio 2. The way Ross liked to record was very different from me. He was into slick LA sounds like The Eagles, and bloody good at it. I was the poor bastard who had the pleasure of carting Little River Band's tapes to and from the studio. It was hard work! Two-inch tapes are heavy, and there were hundreds of them. I'd be endlessly climbing upstairs and downstairs, upstairs and downstairs. No wonder I hate the band's records. It's well-produced, middle-of-the-road crap. Little River Bland! Well, that's the way I saw it.

I was up myself: a pot-smoking, acid-gobbling smart-arse who thought he knew it all. Roger was forever telling me off, and rightly so. 'This job isn't about glory and all that shit!' As the youngest engineer you did whatever you were told, and they were often crappy jobs – like making two hundred cassette copies of Kamahl's latest album, *Let It Be Me*.

I could think of nothing worse. Let it be someone else!

32

It's hard to believe now but the cassettes were all dubbed in real time. So I learnt the art of bludging and would hide up in the roof, trying to get out of work I didn't want to do.

T.C.

The roof of Studio 1 was a huge sandpit – a false ceiling layered with sand to trap low frequencies, which over the years became quite dirty. It was a great spot for lunch, or a wee nap.

Roger's office was also in the roof, next to an exhaust fan. Often at lunchtime the legendary Ron Tudor would join him for a couple of whiskies. Ron ran the independent label Fable Records and was a judge on the television shows *New Faces* and *Young Talent Time*. It was very funny eavesdropping on the two of them, especially when Roger would tell Ron my latest pathetic excuse for being late. I came up with some shockers! They would piss themselves laughing, so it became hard not to continue the game. I spent the entire drive to work trying to think of what to say.

You see, I'd be at the studio twelve hours a day, and seven days a week if I could.

But never before 9.30 a.m.

I got into trouble about it every day – Roger wanted me at the studio at nine o'clock in the morning. To get there at that time I had to leave home at 7.45. But if I left at 8.45, or maybe even a little later, I could get to the studio at 9.30. So instead of an hour's drive in peak traffic, it would be half an hour. I tried so hard to explain. 'I'm here until eight or nine o'clock at night without fail,' I argued. 'Can't I save myself half an hour of peak-hour driving?' It wasn't to be. Roger was a hard taskmaster.

I would hide in the roof for a year before they found out. I think it was Ernie Rose who finally cottoned on, and he was the last person you wanted to catch you. Luckily there was another good hiding spot in the basement car park.

T.C.

Living in my parents' garage was fine, up to a point. It was made of compressed cardboard, and possum piss had created large holes in the roof. I remember coming home from the studio at five o'clock one morning. The possums were returning from the night's foraging, the mama with a baby on her back, walking along the wire that led to the light in the middle of my room. Annoyed, I picked up an ashtray and hurled it at them. In response she pissed everywhere and the smell sent me out.

I moved into a small flat with Chris Thompson in Parkdale. The fair dinkum odd couple. I was a slob and he was quite neat, by comparison. Chris is one of the nicest people you can meet. He had finished school and got a job at the ABC learning to be a sound engineer.

What a square!

Chris Thompson at Christmas, 1976. Image courtesy of the Cohen family.

Chris learnt technically. It took him longer to get good at it, but he's good at it in a different way than me. I like that we have opposite methods of working. Everyone has to find their own way. And technically, I still don't know a lot.

We smoked shitloads of pot and spent the odd weekend on acid, tripping all night. We'd leave gifts for the neighbour's garden gnomes and watch them come out to collect their morning paper, puzzled at these strange offerings to their red-hatted friends. It sent us into fits of laughter. When the Jehovah's Witnesses knocked at the door, we invited them in. The floor was covered in melted candles. To their credit they had a go at preaching to us until the subject of devil worship was brought up. They seemed pretty keen to bugger off after that, but still left copies of *The Watchtower*.

T.C.

Lobby Loyde's music wasn't fooling around. His band Coloured Balls were hard rocking, but he was the last person I would describe as a sharpie. He was a full-on hippie.

Lobby was all about peace and love.

He was in Studio 2 recording *Obsecration* with Graham Owens. I'd got to know Lobby really well – in fact, he was my dealer. 'I buy my hash from Lobby Loyde!' I thought that was quite the claim to fame. Hash and Buddha sticks were Lobby's specialty. Back then you could buy an ounce of hash, which was the size of a cigarette packet, for eighty dollars. Later an ounce became the size of a matchbox and smaller. It's probably the size of a thumbnail now. Most peculiar. Weights and measures must have changed over the years.

Lobby was working with a singer named Mándu, who had recorded a concept album, *To the Shores of His Heaven*, with Ernie the year before. Mándu had a beautiful, sweet voice. I didn't know the man well, but saw him as a mentor. He gave me some great advice about driving: 'Just relax. Stay in the centre and don't worry about changing lanes. Drive easy and peaceful.' That may sound banal, but he was right. On a three-lane high-way it's the only way to go. Stick to the middle lane.

T.C.

It was one of my jobs to keep Armstrong's clean, and I did my best. There was a spiral staircase to Roger's office which we'd all slide down. I polished the handrail, not realising it would result in Roger going at 1000 miles an hour when he sat on it in his slacks. The poor man came a cropper! I wasn't proud of that and am lucky he didn't break his neck. If Roger didn't exist, the consequences would have been terrible.

Why did he keep me on?

I was a very naughty boy and came close to being sacked many times, especially when I got the biggest client's niece stoned. That was a terrible day. In my defence, she told me she was eighteen and smoked dope all the time. 'Great,' I said. 'Let's go and have a joint out the back.' I rolled it with Buddha stick, potent buds from Thailand. It turned out she was a fourteen-year-old schoolgirl. I gave a grovelling but sincere apology and Roger forgave me. I didn't get the sack – it would be a few more years before he did that.

Beyond Morgia

(1975)

Shindig was an all-ages gig at the Mordialloc Life Saving Club on Sunday nights. I'd seen dance band The Paul McKay Sound perform there long before I started working at the studio.

Little did I know I'd record a single for them.

My title as the stereo dubbing boy was just below that of engineer. I'd record demos and the engineers would come in and record it again, to create the finished product. But there comes a time to move on and at the end of 1975 I got my opportunity, courtesy of Ron Tudor and Fable Records. The first single I recorded was 'Take You Where the Music's Playing' by The Paul McKay Sound, a cover of The Drifters' song. It was a great experience.

The single was released in November and didn't break any sales records, but it wasn't about that. Ron gave people a chance to make records. They weren't expected to be the biggest hits of all time. As I recall it's a crappy recording and mix, but to those who wouldn't know, it sounds like a record. I'd got my break! Thanks, Ron.

T.C.

Live recordings were a big part of the 1970s and '80s. AAV had a small mobile recording truck filled with two 24-track tape recorders and a great big mixing desk. Ernie Rose was the man with that. Paul McCartney and Wings played the Sidney Myer Music Bowl on 13 and 14 November, they hired the truck and I had the pleasure of being an assistant on the recording.

Yes, I met a Beatle.

After sound check everyone went to dinner while I stayed in the truck sitting guard. The door burst open and a couple of big boofheads leapt in, and behind them was Paul McCartney! Fuck me. I got the fright of my life. A bloody Beatle, and smoking a spliff the size of a baseball bat if you don't mind. 'M-M-M-Mr McCartney,' I stammered. He was friendly and asked about the Optro equipment and how the show was being recorded. I dribbled explanations as best I could for a few minutes until, thank god, he left before I had a heart attack. I was so nervous.

When it was showtime I watched the band play from the side of the stage. There was something funny going on – the drummer seemed out of it, maybe drunk. Paul smiled at the audience, but as he turned around his face became a contorted scowl. 'Fucking get it together!' he snarled at the drummer, then turned back to face the audience with a smile.

I had some of the best times in the AAV truck. We recorded The Doobie Brothers that summer at Festival Hall. They were great musicians. Before the gig I watched the band play a spirited game of baseball out the back with a plank of wood and rolled-up gaffer tape. 'Hey man, home run!' True to name, there were many doobies in hand.

T.C.

In December I had three weeks' holiday and took off around Australia in the Mini. It's not the sort of thing you'd do if you knew anything about driving around this country. I only got as far as northern Queensland, but I had a lot of fun.

In Queensland magic mushrooms grow to the size of dinner plates. Big and white, with gold speckles on top. Not the slimy little toadstools you find in colder climates. I filled a bucket to bring back for my mates and packed them in honey as a preservative – whether that works I still don't know. I ran out of money driving back and found that eating the mushrooms destroyed my appetite so, as a result, was tripping the whole time. I know, I'm lucky to be alive, but Minis are like dodgem cars: you can hop out of the way of trouble, as long as your reflexes are working. I never found hallucinogenics too bad for driving. Occasionally I couldn't tell what reality was, but I wouldn't drive if I was that far gone.

My car broke down on the Princes Highway south of Sydney. There wasn't much traffic so I parked on the side of the road, put up the bonnet and waited for someone to stop and help. I sat there all day! Finally I realised that I was at the top of a mountain, so I put the car in neutral and rolled down into a little country town. The petrol station mechanic came out, adjusted the carburettor and on I went. When I reached the coast I noticed a police car parked in a side street. I turned and looked, which was a bad move. Our eyes met. Mine must have been as red as the Mini van, so I was promptly pulled over.

'What's that?' the copper said, pointing at the bucket in the back.

'Soup!' I replied.

The police rang Sydney to find out what drug I was carrying.

'Psilocybin.'

'Silly-what?' the copper said as he tried to write it down.

'Psilocybin.'

'What? How do you spell that?'

They stuck me in jail for the night. It was rank – a concrete box out the back of the police station. There was a blanket on the floor and a bucket in the corner. A thick black cloud of mosquitoes hovered 2 feet below the ceiling, making quite a racket. Fortunately, the cops didn't find the Mandrax I had hidden in the side pocket of the Mini, so I got a good night's sleep. I drove back to attend court months later. 'I don't know why you young people don't just take arsenic and be done with it!' the magistrate said. '$100 fine!'

T.C.

Ian 'Molly' Meldrum is one of the greatest people I've ever met. As a music producer he's a genius. We first worked together in April 1976, when I was just eighteen. He taught me so much, though he wasn't meaning to.

Molly wanted an engineer for a young band he'd found from Perth called Supernaut. Why me? I have no idea, but it worked out nicely. 'I Like It Both Ways', written by singer Gary Twinn and brothers Chris and Joe Burnham, is a funny song about a guy who doesn't know where he wants to put it. Most educational. You can understand why dear Molly thought it was good. He was like a moth to a flame.

LISTEN
'I Like It Both Ways'—Supernaut

'I Like It Both Ways' is a recording of a band that couldn't play. We had trouble getting it down and if you listen closely you can hear it go in and out of time, all the time. Fair enough, they were pretty young. I tried to guide the band to play better, which was me learning to be a producer. We must have done twenty takes. Finally I gave up as it wasn't going to get any better. Thankfully they had Molly because he came and put the magic into it.

T.C.

Molly told me stories he had heard about the recording of The Beatles' *White Album* that have stayed with me for life. I listened to everything, working hard to understand his doctrine. And Molly's secret?

Exaggeration.

If you listen to the *White Album* now on good speakers you'll hear exactly what I'm talking about. There's no flat bits, everything in the mix jumps out and grabs your attention. It hits you in the bloody face. When mixing, people get too sensitive, they fiddle about listening on studio monitors and get the balance sounding even. Don't. Be dynamic. Keep the action up and push the extremes. Turn things up louder than is considered tasteful. It might sound like you should pull it back, but resist that temptation. Turn it up a bit more! You'll find that when the song makes it to another medium, into people's cars and homes, there's a presence. The mix is moving, it's alive.

What a lesson. It took me a long time to get any good at putting it into practice, but I still use it today. Exaggeration works just as well for pop music as it does for Nick Cave. Molly was absolutely right.

T.C.

I'd never seen anything like it. He was standing on his chair conducting the mix. 'More phasing!' Molly yelled, waving his arms about. 'More! Louder! Louder!' It sounded ridiculous, the volume was up full.

Phasing is a sound effect made famous in Australia on Russell Morris's 'The Real Thing', produced by Molly. The effect that engineer John Sayers achieved on that recording is a lot of work. You needed two tape machines, or maybe more if Molly was in charge. He'd want an army of tape machines! By sending the mix to two machines and varying the motor speed of one, John got that swooshing sound. Phasing. On 'I Like It Both Ways' I used a rack unit, the Eventide Instant Phaser, to achieve the effect. It was much easier.

I like to be loud, but there's only so far you can go.

Back then there weren't FM stations, only AM, so to check the mix you'd switch to mono. Molly kept complaining there wasn't enough separation between instruments. When mixing, you have the master volume up full and the other faders hovering around the middle somewhere. As I kept bringing each instrument up, I was pulling the master fader back because there was too much level. I was running out of headroom, which is no good because you lose dynamics. So I'd pull everything down, put the master fader back up and start again. But an hour later everything would be exactly where I had it before. I was freaking out and didn't know what to do, so I ran to Roger Savage for help.

Roger came in with a cigarette in his mouth.

'Hmm, separation …' he mused. Grabbing a couple of cords, he plugged them into the patchbay and announced that he'd patched in a separator. Molly was most impressed. He sat at the mixing desk listening and adjusted the faders Roger had labelled 'Separator'.

'Oh yes, yes,' he replied. 'That sounds much better.'

Of course the faders didn't do anything, and there's no such thing as a separator! Sorry, Molly. 'I Like It Both Ways' was released in May and was a big hit. I gained some notoriety, and more work. I never received any money, but it wasn't about that.

T.C.

Native Americans take peyote and have a chat to a wolf or an eagle. I took it and recorded an album for Lobby Loyde – more specifically, the music for his recently completed science fiction novel *Beyond Morgia*. Lobby had great ideas and his philosophies were fantastic.

The album was supposed to be recorded by Graham Owens. I turned up at AAV one weekend in June while the band was rehearsing in Studio 2. I was tripping quite heavily and shared the drugs around. It was the sort of stuff that lasted two or three days. 'How about you mic us up?' Lobby suggested. 'We'll record what we do.'

I put up microphones everywhere.

AAV had a cheap mic hanging from the studio roof so we could hear what musicians were saying. It made the drums sound tough, so I left it on and started recording. Lobby was overjoyed, it sounded fabulous.

LISTEN
'Return to Ether' — Lobby Loyde

One roll of 2-inch tape recording at 30 inches per second lasts for about fifteen minutes. I helped myself to eight. Each tape was a jam, which became the basis of the album. Oh boy, did I get into trouble!

New tape was really expensive, even back then. I never knew what happened to *Beyond Morgia*. Lobby went to London and took the tapes with him. I didn't even know we finished the album, it was only when it was released thirty years later as *Beyond Morgia: The Labyrinths of Klimster* that I found out. It's bittersweet. I shouldn't have used all that tape, but some good music might have gone begging.

T.C.

I smashed the Mini and bought a Kombi van from a Baptist minister for a thousand dollars. It was a bad decision – I spent another thousand dollars trying to get it to work. It was a 1957 model, with the split windscreen, and was so old it didn't have a fuel gauge.

I sold it a year later and was paid fifty dollars, for the tyres!

By the time I got together with Supernaut to record their debut album it was just me and them. None of us had a clue what we were doing, we were just a bunch of naughty kids given a playground. Supernaut were a bad Led Zeppelin copy. They had the hair, they had the riffs, and girls would come in after school to hang around and get wild. There was a microphone in the vocal booth next to the control room and I won't say what went on in there, but it was five-star pornographic! I wonder if a tape exists. Everyone was having a ball.

In the end, more time was spent on the song 'I Like It Both Ways' than Supernaut's entire album. But it was fun. We tipped the studio cigarette machine upside down to get the money out, let off the fire extinguishers. The album is shit but that's beside the point.

Dreams of a Love

(1976)

I never use headphones in the studio. It's deceptive and can make your mix sound better than it actually is. I sometimes wonder though what might've been for The Ferrets if I had.

The band came to Melbourne for a midnight-to-dawn demo, which was recorded live and mixed that night. I was blown away. Their music was unique, with all sorts of weird influences. The next day I was playing it loud in the dubbing room making cassette copies for the band. I was really excited. Unfortunately, so was Molly. He came running down the corridor, shouting, 'That's it! That's it! I've found the next Beatles!' From that moment, the band was doomed.

The Ferrets began recording *Dreams of a Love* in July. It was Billy Miller, K.D. Firth, Dave Springfield, Phil Eisenberg and Ian Mawson. Their original drummer, Ian Davis, was in jail in Sydney, so Rick Brewer from Zoot joined the band.

Molly called us to a 9 a.m. production meeting at his house, which was quite a spectacle. When we arrived he was still in bed. He got up and made a scotch and Coke, then put on some records. Molly plays music very, very loud. Suddenly he started dancing about the room shouting at us. I sat there terrified. What the fuck was going on? No one could understand a word he was saying, so he pulled down a Russell Morris 'The Real

Thing' gold record from the wall and started playing it. We were startled. The speakers went *CRACKLE-CRACKLE-CRACKLE*. I think he was trying to explain good production, certainly not good sound!

I quickly became friends with the band. We played *Sgt. Pepper's* through the huge monitors in Studio 1 at AAV, and learnt Derek & Clive's album *Live* by heart. Listening to *Sgt. Pepper's* was exciting, and an education. The speakers were like microscopes and enlarged the music. I'm glad I didn't record that album as it would have been too difficult. How engineer Geoff Emerick managed with only two 4-track recorders is, to me, alchemy.

T.C.

One of Molly's great insights into the psychology of the recording process is to make it an event. His only drawback was a desire to party, which could distract from the actual business of recording.

Sometimes you get an image in your mind you wish you could erase. I saw things when recording *Dreams of a Love* I can never forget. Drag queens would appear in the studio in the middle of a session. They were all beautiful people, lovely without fail, but quite mad. One had just arrived back from a sex change in Scandinavia. 'Have a look!' she said, hitching up her skirt. I was shocked! There were stitches and colours unseen on the human body.

Rick Brewer would host Mandrax parties, though no one can recall much about them. One time a 6-foot-tall Māori drag queen dropped her handbag on the studio floor and pills spilt out all over the place. Billy Miller's three-legged dog looked up at her, panting. 'Do you want a Mandy, love?' she asked, with no idea it was a dog. I woke up in the basement car park in the back of my Kombi and all I could see was bricks. I thought I'd been bricked in.

T.C.

I would take acid and drive to Apollo Bay. It was wonderful. I'd sit on the beach and watch the sunrise, then drive back again. LSD was very pure in the 1970s, totally different from anything since. Not that I've had any for years.

The Swiss chemist Albert Hofmann invented lysergic acid diethylamide (LSD) in the 1930s. The CIA got hold of it and did some experiments, but of course it ended up with the hippies in the mid-1960s. A friend of The Ferrets sent over an envelope of 'brown barrels' from London. We were sitting around having breakfast when they arrived. 'I'll try one!' I said.

Oh boy, that was an intense couple of days.

I can understand why some people think tripping is a religious experience. I wandered around the Royal Botanic Gardens and it was spectacular. The hills turned to liquid, rainbows shot into the air – just like The Beatles' animated film, *Yellow Submarine*. When someone asked me where the duck pond was all I can remember is them running away in fear. God knows what I said. Maybe it was my eyes, big black holes staring back at them.

I shouldn't harp on about it. Don't do drugs, kids, they're very bad for you.

T.C.

I learnt early on not to use big studio monitors for mixing. They're good for recording but not to mix on. Nearfield monitors are what you want, a couple of good speakers close, so not too much interferes with what you're hearing.

Dreams of a Love was produced by Molly – when he was around. He was overseas with *Countdown* most of the time and would turn up every few months, say, 'No, no, no, not good enough. Do it again!' then disappear. We had no idea what we were supposed to be doing and ended up with unlimited use of the studio. It was great, we got the chance to experiment.

LISTEN
'Dreams of a Love' – The Ferrets

We wasted hours and Michael Gudinski at Mushroom Records was freaking out. The album was costing him so much money! I remember spending an entire day playing with the coloured lights in Studio 1 just to record Billy's grandmother's clock chime five times, *DING-DING-DING-DING-DING*. You can hear it at the end of the album. Roger Savage's office looked down into the studio. He was standing at the window watching in absolute bewilderment.

T.C.

Codral cold tablets used to have an orange pill in the middle which was ephedrine. If you took enough your skin would crawl. It wasn't pleasant, more a necessity. It would certainly keep you awake.

When mixing, it's best to get it right the first time, but occasionally, if you've got the luxury of a good budget, you can perfect it. Or go mad trying! We did hundreds of mixes for The Ferrets. Molly meant well but pushed things too far. In hindsight it would have been better to leave the band to their own devices. Acid or no acid, they would have come up with an impressive album in a couple of weeks. Instead, the recording went on and on and on.

That's when problems start.

The Ferrets had an old crazy dude on piano, Ian Mawson. He was fantastic. Unfortunately, Molly decided Ian didn't fit the image of a pop band, so he sacked him, and Billy's sisters, Jane and Pam, came in, because they were girls. It caused a rift. Molly wanted to be more commercial than the band did. There was infighting, as there always is. 'Billy's gone off madly,' some said. 'He sees stars.' It was the end of the beginning.

T.C.

Ian Davis was a very funny character, and a great songwriter. He co-wrote some of The Ferrets' songs with K.D. Firth, including their one and only hit, 'Don't Fall in Love'.

Ian didn't have much time for the music business.

47

The A side of The Ferrets' single 'Lies' was written by Ian and K.D. It was a big Eagles-type guitar production which Molly had spent hours on – about two hundred by my calculations. The B side 'Don't Fall in Love' was a different situation altogether. It was recorded and mixed in just eight hours.

LISTEN
'Don't Fall in Love'—The Ferrets

If you've ever wondered why there's no snare drum on 'Don't Fall in Love' it's because Rick Brewer forgot to bring it! What happened was everyone dropped a trip. It was midnight by the time we arrived at Rick's house, so we threw one down his throat and were back at AAV within the hour. By nine o'clock that morning 'Don't Fall in Love' was done. We played it to Molly. He said, 'Yeah, that's great', and it became the B side. We had no idea it would be a hit.

'Lies' was released in June 1977. The pop radio station at the time, 3XY, didn't play the A side but played 'Don't Fall in Love' instead. Next thing, The Ferrets had a number one record. Go figure.

T.C.

Dreams of a Love wasn't coming out the way Molly wanted, but it was never going to. He kept working on it and working on it, a little bit more than he should and it ended up a bit of a mess.

Nicky Hopkins and Bobby Keys toured Australia in July with Joe Cocker, and Molly arranged for them to play on the record. It was purely for their names because they weren't particularly interested, at least Nicky wasn't. He was so drunk I don't think he even knew where he was. Nicky had played with everyone – The Kinks, The Rolling Stones, The Who, John Lennon. It was sad. Every time he fell off the piano stool two roadies would pick him up and put him back on again. Bobby Keys did a little sax solo on 'You Belong with Me', which was great. I loved his playing with The Rolling Stones.

By the time the final tracks were mixed there was barely any sound left on the tapes, they were so worn out. I kept getting sacked by Molly and reinstated, so Ian MacKenzie would take over. He was a very laid-back character, which is a good temperament to have for the job. Nothing much flustered him, not even Molly, and that's really saying something!

Molly could get quite hysterical.

One night he put masking tape all over his face. We drew eyes and a mouth on him and I took a photo with my cheap plastic camera. It's on the album's inner sleeve. The producer: 'Willie Everfinish'.

T.C.

These days artists attend mastering sessions, sit on the couch up the back and nod their heads. It's a shame no one was onto it back then because they would have really enjoyed it. The cutting lathe was a spectacle, a huge turntable with strobe lights. It made a horrendous noise, sucking up lacquer cut by the hot needle.

We mastered *Dreams of a Love* at Festival Records in Sydney. I was over-awed by the occasion. By then Molly was really panicking. There was no more mixing, so he tried making last-minute edits, swapping small pieces of tape from one mix to another. It was unfortunate – the whole sound would change for a couple of bars. We flew back to Melbourne and I drove us home from the airport. With no money we couldn't pay to get out of the car park, so I got Molly to lift the boom gate at the entrance while I drove the Kombi against the traffic. Then I ran out of petrol. We wandered around the suburbs with a petrol can and of course everyone recognised Molly.

Dreams of a Love was finally released in October 1977, fifteen months after it started. The album cover wasn't even ready! What an experience. Molly's natural feel for pop music and how to exaggerate sounds had taught me most of what I needed to know. I can never thank him enough.

Fame at Any Price

(1977)

When I joined The Ferrets on tour I had very little live experience. I had mixed their hit single 'Don't Fall in Love', but tune a PA? Give me a break. That's a mystical craft best left to the road crew.

The Tiger Room was at the back of the Royal Oak Hotel in Richmond. It was only small but a great place to mix. By the end of the year it became known as The Tiger Lounge. I would insist on setting up a monstrous double 4-way Nova Sound PA for The Ferrets. With two 50-inch bass speakers it was heavy and ridiculously powerful, not to mention totally inappropriate. It took up half the room! The sound was awesome and people loved it, getting drunk on the bottom end, bass drum rupturing their spleens at 700 million decibels. The road crew, however, was furious.

'Wanker!' they said.

I was a twenty-year-old pop-star mixer who travelled with the band.

T.C.

After Radio 3EA, Studio 3 at AAV was empty. In time it would become a mixing room, but for years it remained a shell, a half-made studio that bands would use for rehearsals. Little River Band's instruments were set up for work on their next album, *Sleeper Catcher*.

Fucking dicks.

I arrived at the studio with The Wombats, Billy Miller's brother's band. We were off our heads and decided to record an album. It was pretty good. The boys strolled in, picked up LRB's gear and away we went. Oh boy, what a stink. I'm afraid sometimes you don't realise the consequences of your actions. This was bad manners of the highest order. By now AAV had started to get sick of me. With Bill Armstrong no longer there, the studio had become more corporate – they'd had enough of arty-farties. There'd be no more using eight rolls of new tape for a Lobby Loyde jam session! I was becoming unreliable: not turning up, disappearing. They gave me the push and I left the studio, no longer a permanent staff member.

T.C.

Talk about working with stars. Blondie's first trip to Australia was a budget Gudinski tour with The Ferrets as support, booked before 'In the Flesh' had become a hit. Nobody had seen anything like it.

Blondie were a great band. Hard New Yorkers, all white skin and black suits. Debbie Harry was absolutely stunning. Watching them sound check was amazing. I stood at the side of the stage in awe, my heart exploding. Clem Burke, wow. Throwing his drumstick in the air, it disappeared above the Palais Theatre stage curtain only for him to catch it in time for the next beat.

'You pussies! How dare you play so badly.'

What? Chris Stein had stopped the band and was shouting abuse. I couldn't believe it, these guys were cooking. But that's the difference, you've got to be really good to make it in New York.

1977 Blondie Australian Tour

Perth Concert Hall, Perth, Saturday 26 November

Apollo Stadium, Adelaide, Tuesday 29 November

The Palais Theatre, Melbourne, Thursday 1 December

The Regent Theatre, Albury, Friday 2 December

Hoyts Theatre, Wagga Wagga, Saturday 3 December

Civic Theatre, Newcastle, Monday 5 December

Town Hall, Lismore, Tuesday 6 December

Her Majesty's Theatre, Brisbane, Thursday 8 December

Town Hall, Wollongong, Saturday 10 December

State Theatre, Sydney, Sunday 11 December

Canberra Theatre, Canberra, Monday 12 December

Morwell Technical College, Morwell, Thursday 15 December

Plaza Theatre, Geelong, Saturday 17 December

T.C.

We met at the Southern Cross Hotel in Melbourne and travelled up the Hume Highway in a Ventura school bus at 20 miles an hour. The Ferrets and me, scruffy long-haired slobs in jeans and T-shirts up the back, and Blondie down front. The driver had two 8-track cartridges – The Village People and Slim Dusty. Quite a selection.

Our tour manager was a half-toothless Irishman named Ray. He would do anything to keep the band entertained. Patting kangaroos, koalas. When we got out of the bus at Glenrowan the whole town came out of the shops to look at the freaks.

'Where's the goddamn McDonald's, man?' the band asked.

Back then, there was no such thing.

Ray was completely mad. He'd piss in a wine bottle and drink it! When he ate a huntsman spider off a motel wall Debbie ran out of the room sick. That was too much. We eventually got rid of him when he ended up in hospital after licking the back of a cane toad to get high. People do strange things to get somewhere in this business.

I had no idea touring was such debauchery. The Ferrets would play their own show on nights off, and at a small pub in Sydney, Clem and Frank Infante jumped up onstage to join them. It was spectacular. They played Rolling Stones' songs so fast The Ferrets could barely keep up!

By now everyone had started to mingle and discovered we had a liking for the same drugs. When the road crew picked up a deal in Sydney, the Brisbane show had to be cancelled. It was mayhem. The little punks in the audience ripped up the seats, Bjelke-Petersen's 'brownshirts' came in waving their batons and it was on for young and old. I believe it's the only show the band ever missed.

I ended up doing Blondie's front of house one night of the tour. The Ferrets were sounding better and when asked to mix them, too, I was chuffed.

T.C.

Richmond Recorders was a small, privately owned studio at 17 Pearson Street, in the suburb now known as Cremorne. The area had once formed part of the Cremorne Gardens amusement park, which by 1864 was operating as a 'lunatic asylum'.

How appropriate.

I first worked at the studio on The Ferrets' single 'Are You Looking at Me?' It was a bad choice. Molly had a habit of hearing a song at a drunken party, leaping up and declaring it a hit. Had he listened to it sober in the office it would have been a different story, but he would get excited and insist it was done. 'Are You Looking at Me?' was released in April 1978. It didn't sell.

I moved to Sydney with the band and lived in a squat. It was a fantastic mansion overlooking the Sydney Cricket Ground, which was overrun with ferals – us. The poms downstairs had ripped out a wooden telephone pole and were feeding it into the fireplace to keep warm, all the way down to the street sign. Cook Road! In Sydney I was an unknown, but The Ferrets had a community of theatre connections from Billy and K.D.'s time in *Jesus Christ Superstar*. Jane kept us all fed on tzatziki: cucumber, yoghurt and garlic. We must have stunk. No one took much care of themselves and a doctor on Oxford Street gave us vitamin B shots to stay alive.

After a few gigs I returned to Melbourne, with a bout of scabies for my troubles. It rained the whole way back. The windscreen broke, and in the early hours we stopped for petrol.

'Have you got any money?'

'No,' I replied.

So we swapped a tow bar and briefcase for some petrol. I sat with a coat over my head, hiding from the rain, wishing I was somewhere else.

T.C.

Scabies is known as the seven-year itch. Mine didn't last long, but I did spend seven years at Richmond Recorders. The studio was run by Tim Stobart and Chris Napper. All intentions were good but it was a difficult place to work, everybody had trouble with the control room acoustics and would prefer to mix elsewhere.

I was the house engineer so I guess I got used to it.

Every new thing you do gives you more experience and knowledge that you can use in later work. The control room at Richmond Recorders was a small, brown padded room. The bottom end sounded thin at the desk, but I found a better frequency response if I leant back toward the wall. So I'd make adjustments. The expensive in-wall monitors were never used, everything was mixed on small Auratone speakers. Or Horrortones as they were known. Big monitors are just for record company executives, like Michael Gudinski.

He ripped me off a few times but never caused much grief. He was too busy dealing with Molly. They were at each other's throats about budgets and deadlines all the time. There's no such thing in Molly's mind, he's never been one for moderation! I was left at Richmond Recorders to work on The Ferrets' unsuccessful second album, *Fame at Any Price*.

T.C.

The Ferrets were special when they first appeared. But things were never the same. It's a bit sad, who knows what might have been? The band was now a four piece: Billy, Dave, Rick and George Cross. They hid under the mixing desk howling with laughter as Gudinski tapped his foot out of time, not a musical bone in his body.

LISTEN
'I Used to Live in This Place' — The Ferrets

We were drug-crazed. I was living in a share house with Billy and Dave on Greville Street in Prahran when we found ourselves working with Molly on the music for an upcoming episode of *This Day Tonight*, a television current affairs program on the ABC. 'On a Slide Going Down' was a report on heroin addiction which went to air in September. What a joke – here we were recording an anti-drug song while people were trying to score.

I started taking anything that came through the door.

'Next!' One band after another, midnight to dawn sessions. It was a blur, quick sessions for quick bucks. Clint Small, Peter Lillie, Au Go Go, Missing Link. One job led to another. Things were about to change and I was stumbling right into it.

T.C.

I was at AAV in November, freelance mixing a live record for Dave Warner. It was on the cheap, which meant 2 a.m. starts.

'Nightrider! Cruising at the speed of fright!'

The noise from Studio 1 was deafening so I stuck my head in to see what was happening. On the screen was the opening car chase from *Mad Max*. Sirens, shotgun, tyres squealing. The monitors were at an incredible volume. It was Roger Savage.

Roger's understanding of sound and timing is genius. By the late 1970s he was mixing for film, and would go on to establish his own successful company, Soundfirm. I stood amazed, but Roger had noticed something wasn't right. Peering through cigarette smoke he kept mixing the scene until a gunshot went off at exactly the right time. I loved watching him at work. It was always so impressive.

Door, Door

(1979)

One band that stood out was The Boys Next Door. I first met Nick Cave, Rowland S. Howard, Mick Harvey, Tracy Pew and Phill Calvert at Richmond Recorders in January. I appeared shoeless, red-eyed and late. As usual. The grand piano was overflowing with bits of metal, microphone stands, anything that wasn't nailed down. 'That should sound interesting,' I said.

It was the start of a great love affair.

I didn't know The Boys Next Door, they were just another band coming to the studio to record. It wasn't like later years when people would ask to work with you, or perhaps not go anywhere near you! Back then I was the house engineer, so they had to work with me. Side one of *Door, Door* had been recorded with producer Les Karsky prior to Rowland joining the band. It didn't go well. Nick was asked to double track his vocals. It's a recording technique that involves singing the songs exactly the same way twice. That's how Karsky knew to make records, but it was never going to work with The Boys Next Door.

Nick had his own way. He'd jump about all over the place, tearing headphones out of the wall. We'd often end up with only one pair left. I didn't give a shit – these guys were going to break new ground and that suited me just fine.

T.C.

One of the most valuable things a band can have is an outside opinion, offering ideas where necessary. When you're close to something and working on it intently you can often miss things that are obvious. Not to say everyone will agree.

Rowland wrote most of the tracks on side two of *Door, Door*, but I wasn't familiar with his earlier Young Charlatans' version of 'Shivers' when I suggested that he sing the track. Two vocals were recorded: one from Nick, and the other Rowland. Finishing late at the studio and feeling wound up, we'd sometimes head out to Tullamarine airport, the only place to get a drink at that time of night. I argued that hearing another voice on the album would provide a good contrast, much like Keith Richards singing the odd Stones track. Nick, however, wouldn't have a bar of it. 'No, I'm the singer. We're not using Rowland's vocal.' I admitted defeat. He's a proud man and didn't want anyone else singing on the record. I still think I was right, the sound of Rowland's lovely deep voice, but Nick's version is pretty good too.

LISTEN
'Shivers'—The Boys Next Door

I became very influenced by The Boys Next Door. I got my hair cut and bought a pair of shoes! I wasn't much interested in the punk thing, but the drugs and ratbagginess of it all was fantastic. For me, it was a chance to get a bit more out of it and be a little less responsible. *Yeah*, I thought. *This is the way to live!*

T.C.

I have a huge amount of respect for Mick Harvey. We taught each other a great deal. Aside from Molly's theories, I learnt more from Mick than I did even from Roger Savage and Ernie Rose. They taught me the technical stuff, but doing things different? Mick had so much to do with that.

Mick was good at describing what he was looking for in a certain instrument or blend of instruments. He was a natural. 'Why are you put-ting reverb on that?' he'd ask. I'd explain it might give the mix depth to push one instrument back or bring another forward. 'Oh yeah,' he'd say. 'Why not try this?' Mick was easy to understand because he never compli-cated things. It was my job to work out where to put microphones to make instruments sound good. He had no idea about that and wasn't particu-larly interested either. Mick just knew what he wanted to hear.

Richmond Recorders was a small 1970s non-reverberant design, acoustically dead. I started to move the drums out of the booth and into the live area of the studio. I'd put microphones in the corners of the room, facing away from the drums, to pick up sounds reflecting off the walls. I tried the technique on lots of instruments. You can get great sounds mixing together three or four ambient signals.

T.C.

On 'The Hair Shirt', Nick sang through a telephone. It was hysterical. He wanted a screechy voice underneath his lead vocal, so I gave him the stu-dio phone. I ran upstairs to the office, picked up the handset and set up a microphone to record the speaker. The sound was piercing. It blew your head off, but combined with the lead vocal it sounded great.

LISTEN
'The Hair Shirt'—The Boys Next Door

Rowland always wanted more treble on his guitar, so I brought in sheets of corrugated iron and made a tunnel covering his amp, with contact mics placed all the way along. It sounded awesome, completely over the top, which was exactly what he wanted. Tin exaggerated the treble frequen-cies. Unfortunately, we couldn't use much of the sound in the mix because it destroyed everything else. I tried the technique on kick drums but it didn't work, it just made the fillings pop out of your mouth. We were experimenting a great deal. Not all of it was brilliant, but it's nice to explore.

The Boys Next Door mixing *Hee Haw* at Richmond Recorders, 1979. Left to right: Tony, Rowland S. Howard and Mick Harvey. Image courtesy of Clinton Walker.

I often drove the band home after sessions, all piled into the back of my Mini. Tracy cracked the back window, the bloody boofhead! After the Kombi debacle I had bought another van. I almost got talked into buying a Mini Moke convertible. Can you imagine them in the back of that?

T.C.

Michael Gudinski lost The Boys Next Door because he couldn't deal with them. Keith Glass took over managing the band and that's when things got interesting. He had played in bands in the 1960s and ran a record store and label called Missing Link.

I became closely connected to the underground scene, but I never followed trends. I still don't and prefer to stumble through blindly. It's good because you can't copy things if you don't know what they are. I'm very grateful to Keith because he brought me fantastic acts to record: The Boys Next Door, Laughing Clowns, The Go-Betweens. At the time,

I didn't listen to much music. I was busy working with the hippies and these were the punks about to emerge from it all. They were a different lot, but I fell into it quite comfortably.

The musicians were the same age as me.

Keith and I worked together for a while. He co-produced The Boys Next Door's *Hee Haw* EP. We respected and understood each other but never became close as a production team. I wish we had, we could have done some good work together, but it didn't come about. After *Door, Door* The Boys Next Door didn't want a producer, just an engineer they could trust. They wanted to express themselves without any rules.

T.C.

I leased a house a few doors down from the studio. It was a miserable place I was supposed to fix up in return for rent. I started painting the walls with a lumpy textured paint that was popular at the time, but I'm no handyman. It probably ended up looking worse.

Never live too close to a studio – that's some advice.

I got sucked into working all the time. Open up, lock up. Day and night. It became a nuisance but a lot of entertainment came my way. Chris Thompson had also started working at the studio. It was a bizarre cross-section of jobs. Skyhooks, Mondo Rock, Joe Dolce. I did recordings with Split Enz in September. They were album demos and a single called 'Things'. It was great to work with the band. Their percussionist Noel Crombie was bonkers! He was the one responsible for their hair and cos-tumes. Noel played spoons and all sorts of strange things.

LISTEN
'Things' – Split Enz

Split Enz were really good musicians. They were slick, which was not what I had expected. Apparently one or two of those demo recordings were used as backing tracks on *True Colours*. I don't know if that's true, it's hard to tell. It would only have been the drums, bass and a bit of gui-tar, with the rest rerecorded.

T.C.

Tim Stobart's business partners kept office hours. My hours were more toward the end of the day until sunrise, so we wouldn't often cross paths. Chris Napper and I didn't see eye to eye.

Chris was a bit too clean living for me and came from a different world. His shtick was commercial recording, like Johnny Young's televi-sion show *Young Talent Time*. It was bizarre, the cast would be at the studio all the time. The kids would arrive at 9 a.m. with songs for the next episode, then mime to their recording on the show. Chris and I had a number of disagreements about it. I'd be at the studio, tired from an all-night session with the punks, and get into trouble for running overtime.

Once I was finishing the razor-blade edits on a mix for The Boys Next Door when the *Young Talent Time* cast and musicians arrived.

'I'll be another fifteen minutes,' I said.

The show's engineer was a real pickle, I didn't like him.

'No,' he replied. 'Not good enough. You're out, our time starts now.'

Apparently I went at him with the razor blade.

'You get out of here or I'll fucking slash you with this!'

Nick and the rest of them started rolling around on the floor laugh-ing. I got my extra fifteen minutes, but doubt I won any popularity contests. I remember chasing a frightened Tina Arena out of the building one morning. We did things like that, just for a joke. What ratbags. What unpleasant little punks.

Breaking Silence

(1979)

Tim Stobart was very down on people injecting drugs. He painted a sign in the toilets – TO HIT IS TO MISS – and drilled holes in the bottom of the teaspoons. It was a practice inspired by cafes on Fitzroy Street in St Kilda. Talented junkies would of course get around this by balancing the spoon at a different angle. Some people even used their sunglasses to mix up in. They tipped them upside down and used the indentation of the lens. That's desperate.

T.C.

The James Freud sessions had been going on for months. I had expected to work on *Breaking Silence* so was quite put out when some Englishman, Frank Owen, turned up instead. *He must be good*, I thought.

He was shithouse!

I couldn't believe it. The band had flown out someone with no experience recording an album. He was a live engineer who sat in a broadcast van getting levels to tape. There was a great panic and James' manager, Barry Earl, was freaking out. The whole album had been recorded and was a total disaster. At the end of the year I was called in to try and fix it up. 'See, told you I could've done better!'

Barry was a dodgy character, the ultimate sleazy used-car salesman. It was almost expected of managers back then. Apparently I took over *Breaking Silence* on the condition he wasn't allowed in the studio. Fair enough. Managers don't fit into the artistic side of the business. It's a different world. Even The Beatles' manager Brian Epstein knew to keep out of the studio, only popping in every now and then.

I played back James' tapes and was appalled. The performances were good but there was no top end on the recording at all. It sounded muffled, as if someone had put a mattress in front of the speakers. The snare drum, an important sound on a pop record, was barely present. There was no clarity, no depth, no space.

T.C.

Some materials have good acoustic properties and some don't. Wood is my favourite, but if you want a hard-sounding reverb then find a concrete cupboard or stairwell. Something with a bright, reflective surface.

The microphone cupboard at Richmond Recorders was a long concrete corridor with pegs and cables hanging from the wall. I clapped my hands. 'CLACK!' It had great acoustics. I found a small Tannoy speaker box and laid it flat in the cupboard with a snare drum placed upside down on top. Gating the original signal from tape, I fed the snare hits to the Tannoy, very loud, so the speaker physically hit the drum. At the back of the room a microphone picked up the treble, creating a new, refreshed sound. I treated other instruments similarly, using different spaces for their acoustic properties, and in the process brought the recording to life. What a clever little prick!

LISTEN
'Modern Girl'—James Freud

I put a lot of work into James' album. I doubt I rescued it all but I was glad 'Modern Girl' was a hit. I thought it might be, but I wasn't interested in that at the time. For me, *Breaking Silence* was an experiment to try to save bad sounds. It gave me a huge confidence boost, and as for the microphone cupboard, that was a revelation and I would use it from then on.

T.C.

Rowland Howard was an amazing man and his performance on 'The Friend Catcher' is one of the most spectacular things I ever saw in a studio. It was just one take, if I remember correctly.

The Boys Next Door recorded the song at the start of 1980 as a backing track with drums, bass, the guitar riff and probably a guide vocal. Rowland then performed a guitar overdub, a feedback noise that went right through the song. He spent a long time setting it up. Every pedal and gizmo known to man was spread out on the floor. There were a shit-load of distortion pedals, including a fluke MXR Blue Box Octave Fuzz which didn't work properly but made a great sound. Finally everything was plugged into a Roland Space Echo, which Rowland didn't know how to operate.

A Space Echo is a tape machine that repeats the sound. An 'intensity' knob determines the number of echo repeats and as you put more sound into it, the noise continues to build. Rowland, being a sensitive fellow, turned every knob up full. The result? Constant noise.

LISTEN
'The Friend Catcher' – The Birthday Party

Rowland barely touched the guitar. He didn't have to because the Space Echo was constantly feeding back. Instead, he started bashing pedals to change the sound. We were laughing our heads off in the control room. He had no idea what he was doing, whizzing around madly in a circle with a cigarette in his mouth and smoke in his face, trying to figure out which pedal to hit next.

'I wonder what this one will sound like?'

Bang! Another bizarre sound, with squealing and howling.

As the song came to an end, Rowland turned and faced the control room, with the smouldering butt of his cigarette still in his mouth. The noise kept going – he couldn't stop it. Eventually he loped into the control room and said, 'Yeah, that'll do.' Rowland never showed much emotion about anything, but he was delighted.

T.C.

In those days we all had a hand on the desk. It was a good way to get the band involved and listening to their mix. Little did I realise I was teaching them. On reflection that was a mistake, I did myself out of work!

Nick Cave was in awe of the studio. He didn't understand how it operated and would try to turn everything up full and ruin the effect, so always left it to me. I would give Mick Harvey a few faders to control, Rowland a guitar and I usually had the vocal. Decisions would involve me and Mick, with Nick putting his two bob's worth in – if he was awake.

'The Friend Catcher' mix is completely manual.

We were all huddled around the desk. I set the mix up and adjusted the level of Rowland's guitar depending on each part of the song. It was turned up, up a little bit more, then down, and back up again. The song itself is reasonably long, over four minutes, and someone made a mistake in the last couple of bars. I think it may have been Tracy Pew. He would sometimes wander off and forget his job, so we went back and started again. I preferred that, rather than edit an ending on. Everyone enjoyed the adrenaline of getting their part in the performance right.

'The Friend Catcher' is one of my proudest mixing moments. I even got a pat on the back from the band, which was most unusual. The Boys Next Door, in particular, weren't the type to offer praise.

T.C.

I'm much happier when musicians have input. I like them to have a vision of how the song should sound, then I can add whatever I'm thinking and together we can make a real mess.

Laughing Clowns was Ed Kuepper's band after leaving The Saints. It was Ed, Jeffrey Wegener, Bob Farrell, Ben and Dan Wallace-Crabbe. I recorded their first EP at Richmond Recorders in February. It was a fantastic session. Bob played his saxophone in the cupboard with a microphone up the other end, just like James Freud's snare drum. It was a great sound. The concrete exaggerated the high-mid and treble frequencies.

LISTEN
'Holy Joe'—Laughing Clowns

The *Laughing Clowns* EP is a superb-sounding record. I'm always grateful to have seen these artists at their most creative and been a part of it. Jeffrey, their drummer, was one of my favourites. He was a purist, the first dude I met who used real pigskins on his drums, and the bugger could play the things. The best sounds always come from musicians, not the equipment. I made a fool of myself years later when I saw Ed play an acoustic gig. I asked him what pedals he was using and he glared back at me and held up his fingers. How embarrassing! I didn't know it at the time, but I was working with legends.

T.C.

I never embraced punk but I did start to wear more black. A girl dressed me up in tight pants and leather jackets which was amusing, for a while. Some liked Chris Thompson and me because we were an introduction to a smorgasbord of musicians. By following us around they'd get to meet all these other drunkards. My girlfriend at the time came back from a holiday and wondered what the hell had happened. I'd suddenly turned into a punk rocker! So she moved out and that was the end of the house on Pearson Street. My budgie, Eccles, died, too, which was very sad. Possibly I forgot to feed it.

Prayers on Fire

(1980)

The Boys Next Door moved to London and I moved to Beverley Hills, 65 Darling Street, South Yarra. It's a beautiful block of flats opposite the Yarra River. How I got a place in a building like that I'll never know.

Beverley Hills was built in the 1930s by the maniac developer Howard Lawson. It's a wild construction, comprising two towers of Hollywood Spanish Mission and Art Deco architecture with spiral columns and archways. My flat was at the bottom next to the swimming pool. There was even an underwater viewing window so you could see people's feet! The lease was never put in my name, so the real estate agent didn't have a clue who I was. They operated out of a big building in South Yarra with tellers, like a bank. I kept going in and paying the rent, so nothing was ever said. The world doesn't work like that now.

T.C.

No one starts out producing records and in the early days it was a combined effort with the band. After a while people start to think you know what you're talking about, then all of a sudden you're a producer.

The band Models were Sean Kelly, Andrew Duffield, Mark Ferrie and Johnny Crash. Their debut album, *Alphabravocharliedeltaechofoxtrotgolf*, is a great example of Richmond Recorders madness at its peak. The music business wasn't as serious in those days. There was a lot more consideration of art rather than budgets. You could waste weeks in the studio if you wanted to. Well, that's the way I thought! Sessions for the album began in July and went on for months. I had an absolute ball. We experimented and that made for interesting results.

LISTEN
'Two People per Sq Km' — Models

Sean had a terrific ear and could create something out of nothing. An absolute genius. Not all the time, but when he hit on something good, it was really good. So, too, Andrew, who would get the most bizarre sounds out of the keyboards and gizmos he used. *Alphabravocharliedeltaechofoxtrotgolf* remains a good album to this day.

T.C.

I am not a musician. I don't know how to play anything, not even the drums! I deliberately avoided learning an instrument because I didn't want to have the skills to be a songwriter.

The music has always come from the artists.

I never put musical ideas on people in the studio. Some producers pick up a guitar and say, 'No, play it like this,' but I didn't want to get into that. You can end up with a heap of records that sound exactly the same. I let artists do their thing. I'll say when a song doesn't work, but I can't and wouldn't be cheeky enough to make suggestions. They're the songwriter, so I tell them to come up with something. It's my job to be an interpreter between the music and the technology. To translate the artist's song and performance to a medium that, when it's replayed, sounds exactly as they would like, or better. I try to capture the sound that's in their mind, not just mine.

I didn't think I had a particular sound, but as it turns out I do. There's a certain style in the way that I work that has my stamp on it. It just happened that way, and surprises me when I hear it in hindsight.

T.C.

I started to get typecast as making tough punk records. So be it. I knew how to get those sounds, so if someone wanted that on their record they'd call me. I recorded Magazine live at Festival Hall on 6 September in the AAV recording truck. The band was really happy and the show was later mixed and released as the *Play* album. That was quite a compliment.

LISTEN
'A Song from under the Floorboards (Live)'
—Magazine

Other artists weren't interested in punk-sounding records at all. The Reels invited me to record the *Five Great Gift Ideas from The Reels* EP at Albert Studios in October. They thought it was a joke to hire the punk rock dude to record beautiful sounds. 'Let him do something nice for a change.'

I got their humour.

Albert Studios was located at 139 King Street in Sydney. The studio had a great sound and the atmosphere was something else. Studio 1 was AC/DC's room. It was a live 1950s-type design, with white perforated acoustic tiles on the walls. Not many bands would record in there as it was reserved for Albert's artists. There was graffiti all over the walls – pictures of Bon Scott's dick, messages to other bands. The Reels recorded in Studio 2, the slick studio. It was not spectacular or unique but worked beautifully. A good-sounding control room can sometimes be more important than anything else.

T.C.

The Reels were Dave Mason, Craig Hooper, Colin Newham, Paul Abrahams, Karen Ansel and John Bliss. They were gentle, decent people and we got along well. Their leader, Dave Mason, was a very talented man. He was innovative.

The Reels didn't try to do anything shocking, they just puttered along in their own way. The single 'According to My Heart' is a cover of an old Jim Reeves country and western hit. It has a fantastic synthesiser line. Craig, their mad keyboard player, was way ahead of his time and getting into technology that wasn't happening yet, like samplers. He was so passionate. You didn't want to make the mistake of sitting next to him on the couch at the back of the studio. He'd be flicking through books of technical data and diagrams 2 inches thick and say, 'Tony, have a look at this!' My eyes would glaze over, as I had no idea what he was talking about.

Five Great Gift Ideas from The Reels came out well. I think I even had a hand in the great 'Quasimodo's Dream', but it was just an overdub session. The recording of that song went on for quite a while. The Reels are one of my favourite bands of all time.

T.C.

Richmond Recorders became the cheap alternative studio to the big commercial AAV. Day after day there'd be someone new coming through the door, like Paul Kelly. I recorded his first EP with The Dots in December, but have no memory of the session. At the time, they were just another small independent band who'd saved up for a recording.

I was flavour of the month, hitting it hard and working fearsome hours, but I never gave switching between projects any thought. As soon as I put the multitrack tape on, I was there with that particular song. My problem was turning up on the right day. Even now people remind me, 'Oh Tony, you did this ...' back whenever it was and I feel compelled to apologise. Sometimes I don't even know who they are. I would work on one hundred different projects in a year while the band did just one, so of course they remember everything. For me, their recording is jumbled in with everything else.

T.C.

Leaving Australia was the best thing The Boys Next Door did. They lived in squalor and experienced all sorts of trouble, but kept at it. Suffer

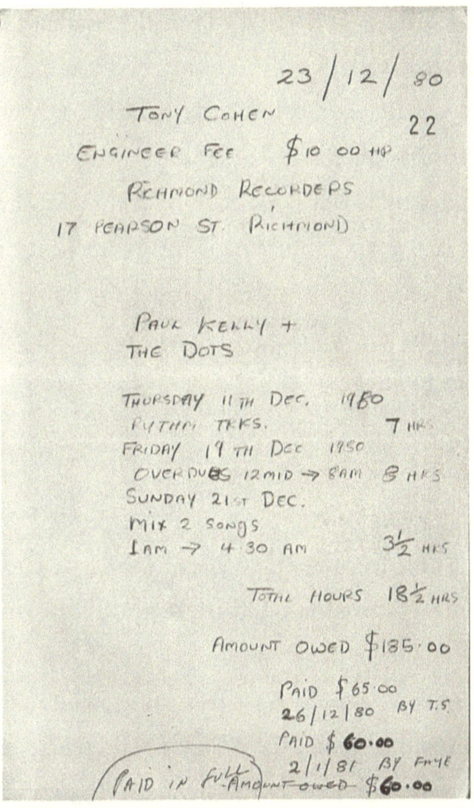

Invoice for Paul Kelly and the Dots' first EP, 1980. Image courtesy of the Cohen family.

for your art? It's true. The band returned at the end of 1980 renamed The Birthday Party, more determined than before.

I was in awe.

The Boys Next Door were a ramshackle outfit that could put together a good recording with effort. It was stumbling in the dark, forcing things to work. The Birthday Party were totally different. All of a sudden the lights were on and everyone knew exactly what they were doing. They were a confident, tight assault band. The rhythm section was thunderous.

LISTEN
'Nick the Stripper'—The Birthday Party

We began recording *Prayers on Fire* in December. The band would always record at that time of year not only because the studio rates were cheap, but because they could leave the cold English winter and come home to visit mum and dad. It worked out nicely for me, too, as Keith Glass had booked Studio 2 at AAV, making it the first time I had worked at the studio in two years. Split Enz were set up next door in Studio 1 recording *Waiata*, released in Australia under the name *Corroboree*, with the English producer David Tickle. He had recorded *True Colours* with the band the year before.

T.C.

Prayers on Fire is a good-sounding album recorded without a lot of flash equipment and I'm proud of that. Split Enz had every piece of effects equipment imaginable piled up to the roof, while we had next to nothing.

The Birthday Party would start recording in the afternoon and go into the early hours. I begged David Tickle for some reverb, so he let me use the studio's lousiest machine, the EMT 240 gold foil plate, at night when his session had finished. I had strict instructions to return it every morning with the settings exactly as they were.

He was acting like a dickhead.

When it came to drugs, most Aussie producers were into stimulants, sedatives and pot, while overseas dudes were all into cocaine. David must have used two-thirds of the coke imported into Australia while he was here. That's alright, I've used about as much of anything else I could find, but cocaine was never one of my poisons. I found it was useless and had a nasty phasing effect on my hearing. It also made you very paranoid. David kept complaining people were coming into the studio at night and changing his settings. Roger Savage even asked if it was us. 'Of course not!' I replied. We were busy working on our own album.

T.C.

The Birthday Party recorded over the holidays, and Split Enz didn't. On Christmas Eve, Tracy Pew ran out of booze and wandered up to Studio 1 to discover twelve bottles of Moët champagne lined up along the mixing desk, a gift from Michael Gudinski to Split Enz. Each bottle was carefully wrapped in Christmas paper, with baubles and individually addressed to the band and their crew.

Tracy scoffed the lot, and made no effort to conceal it.

Strewn all along the corridor from Studio 1 was wrapping paper, baubles and corks, a trail leading to twelve – now empty – bottles in Studio 2. It was hilarious. As he opened each bottle Tracy would complain, 'Ugh, this stuff is fucking horrible!' then proceed to drink it all. I doubt it went down well with Gudinski either. Oh well, it serves Split Enz right for taking a day off.

By then Nick didn't want much to do with Rowland's songs, other than sing them. 'Ho-Ho' was written about a fart. 'The sick wind blows ...' Nick sang the track but I successfully suggested we use Rowland's version on the album. From then on, however, Nick was the singer. I think it was his strength of character that made Rowland give in. You just couldn't argue with Nick. I remember when mixing 'King Ink' I had a reverb on his voice which was supposed to come off before a big wail, but I pulled the faders down too soon. It sounded weird. He was wailing among this reverb when suddenly it went dry.

'I've got to do that again,' I apologised.

Nick insisted it stay and in hindsight he was right. He always liked errors. Happy accidents, I'd call them – luck. They're not details everyone would notice, but we did.

T.C.

The Crystal Ballroom was a well-known venue at the Seaview Hotel on Fitzroy Street in St Kilda. I did plenty of work in those places, but never went there much otherwise. Actually, I didn't go out at all. I was too busy in the studio.

I sometimes worried about my ears and wasn't keen on seeing punk rock bands live. When the sound was too painful I would stand outside. How Rowland Howard wasn't deaf before he departed I have no idea. His guitar sound was fucking awful! Not just ear-bleedingly loud, but mid-range frequencies that hurt. Imagine a jumbo jet in a room with the engines on full blast, except all the bottom end has been taken out.

God bless him.

On New Year's Eve I recorded The Birthday Party playing at The Ballroom. I was sitting in a 2-tonne Avis rent-a-truck parked out the back. It was equipped with a mixing desk, Teac 4-track tape machine and a couple of speakers. Nick appeared in the truck before the show to have a hit of speed. The band was onstage waiting, and through the microphones we could hear Mick Harvey calling out, 'Nick, where are you?' He struggled to find a vein and in the end ran onstage with blood dripping down both arms. The punks cheered, 'Yay, great, Nick. We love it!'

Around midnight, with the band still playing, drunk yobbos started rocking the truck. I thought it was going to end in tears and held onto the speakers and tape machine to keep the recording going. Fortunately the drunkards got chased off, or became bored, and the tapes lived. As I remember it was a pretty poor gig.

Cut Lunch

(1981)

Treble horns blasting at you is unpleasant, but loud with a lot of bottom end is excellent. I saw AC/DC perform at the Sidney Myer Music Bowl on their *Back in Black* tour in February. It was the best. The bass drum was so loud it created a vacuum. After every kick the PA subwoofer would recoil, sucking the air out of the venue. There were twenty empty seats in the middle of the audience.

People had to move because they couldn't breathe!

My flat at Beverley Hills was nearby, half underground and a bit dark. I thought it was good but Billy Miller hated it, so much so it inspired him to write 'I Want to Live in a House'. The song appears in the movie *Starstruck* and was produced by Molly Meldrum. Unfortunately Beverley Hills didn't end well. I had a bust-up with my girlfriend after she noticed some inappropriate marks on my arm. I was badly addicted to amphetamines.

It marked the beginning of a desperate period for me. I moved out of the flat and my drug dealer moved in. That bastard followed me everywhere.

T.C.

I began working with The Go-Betweens in April. It was a lost weekend. I woke in a hotel room with Keith Glass hassling me to get out of bed.

'Where am I?' I asked. I had no idea, or how I'd got there.

'Sydney,' Keith replied. 'You're doing The Go-Betweens' record.'

So he wheeled me off to Trafalgar Studios in Annandale and I met Grant McLennan, Robert Forster and Lindy Morrison for the first time. They were lovely. We recorded three songs: 'Your Turn, My Turn', 'World Weary' and 'It Could Be Anyone'. I spent a long time on drum tunings with Lindy. She was green and lacked confidence, but we worked it out. It's important to not just tune the drums, but to tune them for that particular player. That was something I hadn't figured out yet.

A band as different as The Go-Betweens threw me, and it took a while to catch up. It took most people a long time. Truth is, The Go-Betweens didn't need a great Oz-rock sound, they were fantastic as they were.

T.C.

I was in a terrible state. When you took speed, you later took heroin, the antidote. If you didn't you'd be awake for days on end and wouldn't know what was what.

It affected me badly.

I remember waking up and all I could see was wood. I thought I was in a coffin, buried alive. Then I realised I was under the grand piano at Richmond Recorders. I'd started sleeping at the studio. It was nice and quiet. I had a blanket, foam and a couple of pillows we used to dampen the bass drum. One Saturday morning an all-girl heavy metal band turned up for a session. For me it was a rare day off and I intended to sleep all day. They started tuning their guitars and suddenly hit a chord.

BLAH!

You should have seen the look on their faces when I crawled out from under the piano with dishevelled hair, unpleasant and abusive. They got the fright of their lives!

I lived at Richmond Recorders for nearly a year, sleeping under the piano. There wasn't even a shower. It's one of the lower points in my life, but the recordings were good, and some were even great. I had a studio to myself to experiment in, which is a luxury you can't find these days.

T.C.

I'd love it if when you pressed the record button wheels started spinning, lights flashed and steam burst out. 'Here we go! Whoo, whoo, whoo!' It could only happen in the control room, of course, or the noise would fuck up the recording.

Models' *Cut Lunch* EP started off as a demo with their new drummer, Buster Stiggs. It's a wild recording with lots of mad experiments, like 'Germ (Teradacity Cometh)'. I was getting tired of Richmond Recorders so started sneaking the band over to AAV in the middle of the night. 'Atlantic Romantic' had been recorded there earlier in the year with Split Enz's Eddie Rayner producing and I still had the keys.

'Is anyone in Studio 1?' I'd ask reception.

'No, it's empty.'

Cool. So in we'd go, straight to the big studio with all the gizmos and flashing lights.

I think Sean enjoyed the mischief of recording at AAV. That's where many of his good ideas came out. We'd clear the desk in the morning, leave the studio in a decent state and disappear.

T.C.

The EMT 250 was the first digital reverb and looked like a prop from *Star Trek*. It was a large black heat sink 3-foot high with coloured levers on top. One lever adjusted the reverb length and another two the low-and-high frequency delay. You can hear the sound on *Cut Lunch*.

LISTEN
'Two Cabs to the Toucan'—Models

When I first started at Armstrong's the only way to create artificial reverb was with a plate, which was a huge sheet of steel suspended in a wooden box. Plate reverb had been introduced in Germany in the late 1950s. You would EQ and delay the send signal, then control the length of the reverb by adjusting a damper. Many people liked that sound. It never did much for me, but it was fun to abuse! The delay we used was a Cooper Time Cube, which was a wound plastic tube – a bit like a garden hose. I was very tempted to open the unit and see exactly how it worked, but imagine if the innards started pouring out and I couldn't stuff it back in? Oh no, too risky.

Tim Stobart bought an EMT 250 for Richmond Recorders in 1981. It cost him tens of thousands of dollars but it was a revelation. Now I could significantly effect the sound.

T.C.

Richmond Recorders had a 400 series MCI console. There must have been more drugs inside it than in the rest of Australia! When I saw it opened up for repairs there was white powder and green shit everywhere.

Tim put a lot of work into the desk by upgrading components and got it sounding really good. When four channels were added it came to life. It was exciting because MCI was the first manufacturer to use automation, which meant the desk could remember every movement.

Startling!

Automation used two tracks of the 2-inch multitrack tape for data. The desk would read from one track while writing updated information to the other. It was great for switching things on and off in the mix, especially if the band you were working with was uninterested. Usually I'd give everyone a fader to move, but now I could do everything myself. That was a great boon – or perhaps it was a curse?

T.C.

I could hear people banging outside but pretended I didn't. Morning was not a good time for me. Finally, I woke up and dragged myself to the door.

'Oh, hello guys!'

It was Pel Mel and they'd just driven down from Sydney.

The band was taken aback, so I must have been quite a sight. Pel Mel were nice, clean-living people. They were not so much a rock 'n' roll band, more a group of friends who played music together. They would stop recording each afternoon to watch the soap opera *Days of Our Lives*. I'd seen a lot of strange things in the studio, but that was a first! The band sat huddled around the television with a cup of tea, while I headed back and forth to the kitchen with my glass of water and spoon.

I felt a mismatch with Pel Mel but we enjoyed each other's company. At least I think we did? I certainly enjoyed theirs. At any rate they weren't complaining, it was a good recording.

T.C.

'Down Under' is not one of my favourite songs but I appreciate the effect it had. Overseas, and more specifically in America, music from Australia was an unknown quantity, but that single changed things.

It was certainly Richmond Recorders' biggest success.

Men at Work began recording *Business as Usual* with American producer Peter McIan in July. Tim Stobart had a new business partner, Chris Gough. He was the money man, something Tim wasn't good at. They were beside themselves when McIan turned up at the studio and didn't like anything. This booking was a really big deal for them, which was later justified when the album made it to number one in America and remained there for months, selling millions of copies. Tim was stressing his head off and hired a whole roomful of equipment, everything that whistled and whizzed, to practically remake the studio.

This sort of behaviour was foreign to me. I never had the authority to march into a studio and make demands, I wouldn't be so rude. But this American guy could do what he liked.

Fuck you, I thought.

I didn't appreciate McIan coming into my territory. I've got ego, don't you worry about that! I was supposed to be the engineer on *Business as Usual*, not just some guy who plugs in microphones and cleans up after them. But that's the way it went. McIan would bang on, telling me how recording should be done and unfortunately he was right most of the time, which made it even more annoying. There's nothing worse than someone you don't like being right. So I played up, and instead of watching him, I started mocking him.

I'm ashamed. I could have learnt a few things.

Tim Stobart, Peter McIan and Tony at Richmond Recorders, 1981.
Image courtesy of the Cohen family.

McIan always went on about 'triangular mic-ing'. It was a technique he had developed that used a pair of overhead microphones and room mics to capture the ambience of a drum kit. Each pair formed a triangle in relation to the snare and he would move them closer or further away – in proportion – depending on the song. I didn't take much notice at the time, but wish I had. He got the best drum sound I ever heard out of that studio.

T.C.

Once Americans moved in, nothing else could happen, the studio was set to their specifications. With all the equipment provided to McIan, no one could fit in there anyway!

The Go-Betweens completed their album *Send Me a Lullaby* at nights in July. I couldn't get a drum sound in the studio, but upstairs sounded fantastic. It was a concrete room of unfinished offices. You can hear the acoustics on Lindy's drum solo in 'Eight Pictures'. I set the band up facing each other, with leads running down the stairs to amps in the studio. Poor bastards, it was the middle of winter and they were up there all night, huddled around small electric radiators. Each morning the microphones picked up the first train from Flinders Street as it travelled past East Richmond station. I was cruel to make them work like that, but they understood.

We had to get the sound.

The Go-Betweens had a strange way of playing, and what they thought was a good take fooled me. I'd hear someone say, 'That's it, that's the take!' and I'd think, *Really?* I kept my mouth shut most of the time because only the band knows if they're getting the song across, or could do better.

Junkyard

(1981)

Chris Thompson was renting a house on Wellington Street in St Kilda with his girlfriend, Jo. It was an ex-brothel and had fifteen bedrooms with big mirrored ceilings and round sunken bathtubs. I'd get the chance to shower when I visited.

What a disgusting creature.

I recorded Hunters & Collectors at Chris's house in August. The band's bass player, John Archer, ran a PA company. I had a lot of respect for him, he understood sound well. We set up in the front room and did 4-track demos of their debut album. It was a basic recording but really good. Hunters & Collectors were an innovative band and the music they were making was different, and in many ways better than their successful albums that followed. I'd certainly never heard anything like it – Greg Perano on percussion banging gas cylinders, tin cans and whatever else he could find. *CLANG! CLANG! CLANG!*

At the time, Chris was overseas recording Paul Kelly's *Manila* album, but that's another story. We would often not cross paths, it's the nature of the business. While I was hammering myself Chris would be recuperating, and vice versa. We were both very busy.

T.C.

I moved my belongings into an upstairs office at Richmond Recorders. I was getting well set-up, but it didn't work out, so I rented a flat with Jo above a newsagent on Glenhuntly Road in Elsternwick.

My drug dealer had a PA which I turned into a recording set-up, with cables running everywhere. One Sunday afternoon I was busy doing demos for The Go-Betweens when there was a loud *bang* at the door. All of a sudden a bunch of heavies appeared and started removing the PA in the middle of the session.

'Hey, I'm using that!' I complained.

These weren't the sort of people you argued with, so we sat watching as everything was carried out the door. I wasn't too surprised, I assumed my dealer was in debt and it was time to collect. Grant and Robert looked particularly nervous, the most terrified 'go-betweens' I'd seen in my life. Needless to say, it was the end of the session.

T.C.

I love it when artists come to you with a clear vision of how their music should sound. It saves me from having to think of something. I will go with whatever they have in mind if someone can articulate it. Unfortunately, that doesn't happen often.

Some bands just don't know what to tell you.

Hunters & Collectors began recording at Richmond Recorders in October and by the following month their album had become a huge fuss at AAV. John Archer set up his PA in Studio 1 and the band performed live in front of an audience. The entire album was recorded that way. There was no applause, the audience members were there to witness a record being made.

LISTEN
'Talking to a Stranger'—Hunters & Collectors

AAV had huge, mobile isolation screens made from lead and fibreglass, probably asbestos too. Healthy stuff! I always make an effort to separate instruments, but it depends what you are confronted with. For

Hunters & Collectors it was impossible. There were so many members, I couldn't find space to isolate them all. To this day I don't know everyone who was in that band. There were brass players, jokers hitting tin cans. Random people just seemed to get up and play things.

T.C.

AAV had a long storage cupboard that ran between Studio 1 and 2. It was made of cement and brick, so very trebly. It had amazing acoustics, just like the Richmond Recorders microphone cupboard, only ten times bigger.

Hunters & Collectors, the band's self-titled debut album, was the first time I used that space on a recording. Doug Falconer's drums were positioned half in the cupboard and half out. It worked beautifully. The hard reflective surfaces provided a natural reverb, while close-positioned microphones gave the drums punch. Greg Perano was in that cupboard too. Can you imagine hitting a gas cylinder with a piece of metal in that space? Ouch, evil stuff.

I am particular about microphone placement. It's determined by how you imagine the track will sound when completed, so there's second-guessing involved. Luckily, I've guessed right a lot of the time.

Skill and practice helps.

Think the guitar should sound in your face? Then get the microphone in close. Those drums should be thundering in the background? Put a microphone back to pick up more of the room. Use your ears and explore the space.

I never thought I was learning. I was just trying to make things sound good. But you learn by accident and in the end recording becomes instinctive. I found I would move a microphone in the studio and, after a while, go out and put it back where it was in the first place. You begin to know.

T.C.

Michael Gudinski has always been a sharp businessman. He may have lost The Boys Next Door, but he realised there was money to be made. There could be a place for this other music, but he didn't want it on his Mushroom label, so he set up White Label Records.

Hunters & Collectors were the first band he signed.

I never understood recording budgets, I wish I had. All I knew was you either had a week in the studio or a month – *Hunters & Collectors* was a month. That was a good budget for a debut album, and a surprise to me. Unfortunately, as the money increases so does the pressure, and that can take some fun away from recording. There's stress and tension, but you learn when to back off and when not to, or you soon find out! For the artists, the record you're making is their life. If you get a vibe that perhaps you should fuck off, then fuck off and leave it to the band to sort things out. It's always been my experience that a bit of drama and a few tears make for a better record.

Musicians are funny people under pressure, we all are. I had a falling out with Hunters & Collectors. Doug Falconer was a doctor. I had a bad earache and perhaps I looked into his medical bag at some stage? Sorry, Dougie, I couldn't resist the stuff. *Hunters & Collectors* was completed by Jim Barton months later. He was an assistant at AAV, as I had been years before.

T.C.

I love bass sounds. What I worked for was a sound that was rich and clear, like John Archer's bass on *Hunters & Collectors*. Tons of bottom end, low subsonic stuff, right up to a piano-like top end that would crack.

The Birthday Party weren't interested in any of that.

When the band returned to Australia in December, Nick Cave knew exactly how he wanted his music to be presented. Even in his bad old days he thought deeply about what he was doing and never went at things willy-nilly. At the start of every session Nick and Mick Harvey would come to me with a brief. It had been agreed that *Prayers on Fire* sounded too slick and pleasant. The group felt they'd made a Little River Band album, so this was to be the complete opposite. 'We want it to sound like trash,' they said. 'A scratchy trebly sound.' That was an eye-opener, but it provided me with a clear image of what the band had in mind. It became the sound of *Junkyard*.

I had to unlearn to record some of the harder-sounding records. It was a challenge because I'd been taught by brilliant engineers like Roger Savage and Ernie Rose. They would capture amazing sounds that were technically perfect, so of course I tried to mimic what they were doing. After having it bashed into me a few times by The Birthday Party, I realised sounds didn't have to be perfect. It took me a while to figure that out.

T.C.

There was a big difference between Armstrong's and AAV. David Syme & Co had bought the studio back in 1974, but it felt like now, all of a sudden, it was a corporate place.

I found that ugly.

We had spent most of the first day setting up when the band started playing 'Big-Jesus-Trash-Can'. They were firing so I quickly hit record. Almost immediately a square in a suit appeared at the control room door holding a clipboard. Quite a few of Rowland Howard's friends were in the room with me, weird punks with lots of make-up, a pretty intimidating bunch. This square looked around and said, 'Stop now, there are too many guests. The only people allowed in the studio are the band and yourself.'

'No way,' I replied. 'If you want to try and stop them, good luck.' It's just as well he didn't because that take ended up on the album.

LISTEN
'Big-Jesus-Trash-Can' — The Birthday Party

The band finished playing and came into the control room. This guy was waiting, about to go right off at them. He looked down at his clipboard and said, 'The only people allowed in here are Mr Cave, Mr Harvey,

Mr Howard, blah blah blah.' Without saying a word, Rowland and his mates closed in on him. Closer and closer. Their eyes probably looked a little menacing. They were fair-dinkum smacked-out punks! Fear came across this guy's face. He'd never met people like this before, let alone spoken to them. He went bright red and backed out the door, pleading, 'Alright, alright. I'll go and speak to the powers that be and see if we can get this cleared up.'

He was gone in a flash and that was the last we heard of any complaints, until someone painted a heart of blood in the toilets while cleaning the syringes. That didn't go down well.

T.C.

It was great to be in Studio 1 at AAV. A huge room and lovely microphones make a big difference, but we abused all that and made the album sound as trashy as possible.

Rowland had the most souped-up, loudest guitar amplifier that existed on earth. The noise it made was so bad it almost drowned out what he was actually playing. I put it in the storage cupboard between Studio 1 and 2, as far away as possible. In Studio 2 Linda George was recording an advertising jingle. The noise from Rowland's amp was so loud it bled into her vocal microphone, without him even playing a note! She didn't think it was very funny. We weren't going to compromise Rowland's sound, so had to wait until the jingle was completed before we could turn his amp back on. It was so loud in there, the microphone I used was probably 10 feet away. The sound made your fillings hurt – it was vicious.

We were really mistreating equipment.

I Blu Tacked contact mics to Phill's cymbals and, unsurprisingly, managed to bugger a lot of those up. They only lasted a few minutes before they were blasted to bits. I mic'd up the exhaust pipe of a car and varispeeded the tape to get the sound of a rocket taking off. We were determined to create something hideous, and went overboard.

T.C.

Phill Calvert was never truly one of them. I mean no offence to him, he's a fine drummer and a fine human being but he didn't fit in. Among that group, even Mick Harvey fit in, but Phill didn't.

It was to do with attitude.

In the early days of recording, Phill had significant input, but by the time of *Junkyard* there was tension. At the start of the recording he found a syringe in his bass drum case and flipped out. Fuck, he was upset – slightly overreacted, I thought – but for Phill it was the final straw. Nick thought it was very funny, and the funnier Nick thought it was the angrier Phill got. He was laughed down cruelly.

Mick Harvey is a clever bastard who can pick up an instrument and play it. He does things by ear and usually, as far as I'm concerned, does the right thing. The jungle tom-tom rhythms on 'Dead Joe' and 'Hamlet (Pow, Pow, Pow)' were Mick's idea. The band had started to write songs in the studio, which was a new development. They wanted to try animal drumming and that was something Phill didn't do. He's more of a technician. So Mick jumped on the drums and it was obvious that this was the way to go. It sounded better.

The seeds had been sown. Nick and Mick were top of the heap, Rowland was out on his own, Tracy was a moon orbiting a planet, and Phill was in the backwaters somewhere, almost forgotten. An implosion was imminent.

Out of Reason

(1982)

Drugs played a big part in music, especially punk. It wouldn't have been the same without them. I became so accustomed to drugs in the studio that they formed part of the equipment and I wouldn't contemplate a session without consuming copious amounts. *Junkyard* is not just an experiment of sound, but of physical ability to cope with drugs. If you play the album now, you can hear something was taken out of us. It's a draining record to listen to, and was extremely draining to make. We hit the edge, made it as far as you could go and still live.

T.C.

The Birthday Party show at the Astor Theatre on 15 January was recorded and released years later as *It's Still Living*, but my memory of it is foggy. I was off my rocker.

Recording *Junkyard* had moved to Studio 2 at AAV. It was gigs, recording, more gigs. The hours we were working were insane. I kept taking drugs to stay awake, the side effects of which are appalling. I don't recommend it to anybody. I had a paranoia attack, a speed freak out, before the Astor show. Everything was set up and ready to go, so Chris Thompson came in and took over the recording. It was a shame, but Chris was delighted. He really wanted to work with those guys.

I don't think I ever quite captured The Birthday Party's sound. On *Junkyard*, Nick overdubbed a vocal here, and something else was added there – once you start adding those fiddly bits, you lose the feel of a band playing live. I didn't have much say. If Nick and Mick wanted to do something, I'd say, 'Cool, let's do it!' We were having a great time doing what we thought we should be doing, when we probably weren't doing what we should be doing at all.

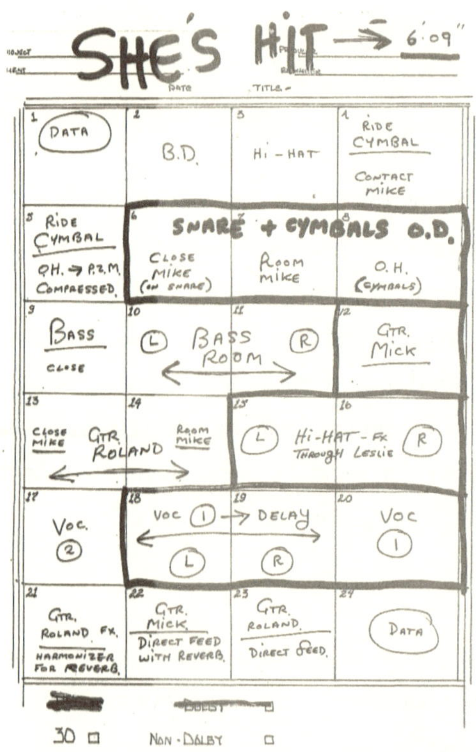

Recording cue sheet for The Birthday Party's 'She's Hit', 1982.

'After the Fireworks' by Tuff Monks wasn't even meant to happen. It was a collaboration between Nick, Mick and Rowland from The Birthday Party and Grant, Robert and Lindy from The Go-Betweens. The bands were touring together and had become good friends, so we used studio time to record whatever we liked. I think that's also how The Go-Betweens' 'Hammer the Hammer' came about. These ideas had to get out, they had to be put down.

LISTEN
'Hammer the Hammer' — The Go-Betweens

T.C.

Tracy Pew was a lovely person and a great musician. A natural. He was great to work with because he never needed a drop-in or retake. Tracy would record his part and that was it. But man, he sure liked to drink.

The Auditronics mixing desk in Studio 2 had just been replaced with a Harrison console, which had a long leather armrest. Tracy was running wild during *Junkyard*, knocking back a couple of wine casks before midday. I went to the toilet and came back to find the entire length of the armrest slashed to ribbons. Tracy was there with his spur cowboy boots, swinging a wine cask back and forth.

'Well, whadareyagonnadoaboudid?' he slurred.

'Nothing, Tracy!' I replied. 'Nothing!'

I was just as fucked up as he was. Drugs and studio work don't mix at all, even though I did it for so long. My record was seven days without sleep. Trying to drive like that was scary, objects would seem to hop onto the road, so I'd sleep at the studio instead. I think we were thrown out of AAV in the end. It's a shame because the mixes could have been much better. Everything culminated in a trashy, nasty-sounding record.

Well, that's what they wanted!

We were zombies by the time we finished *Junkyard*, a complete mess. I remember the band leaving to go back to England and none of us could even talk. There were just a few grunts to say goodbye.

T.C.

Pel Mel were an underrated band, they were doing weird and interesting shit. *Out Of Reason* was recorded in June at ATA in Sydney, Col Joye's studio. The band used very little fancy equipment, nor did they seem to want it.

They were spartan.

Pel Mel had battery-operated Casio keyboards a foot long. Small things can sound big, and as you go down in size the sound can often get bigger. I put the keyboards through a Marshall amplifier – it sounded fantastic, tough and present. All the keyboards were recorded that way. I would sometimes combine a direct input (DI) from the instrument for clarity, but it was mostly the amp. I love DI'd guitars mixed with amps. I add just a hint, enough to hear the sparkle of the strings.

LISTEN
'Screaming Heart'—Pel Mel

Many bands make the mistake of trying to put too much on a recording. You should be able to get a small number of instruments sounding good. If you can, you're going to make a much better record, unless of course it's a textured piece like 'The Mercy Seat', but that's another story altogether.

T.C.

The Reels had lots of engineers. It was usually Bruce Brown, the main engineer of Studio 2 at Albert's, but they liked working with me, so I would crop up here and there. I worked with the band live in 1982, just after they'd released their album *Beautiful*.

There were only three members of the band at that time – Dave Mason, Craig Hooper and Stephan Fidock – so there were sounds they couldn't perform live. They didn't try to hide it. Instead, the band put a Tascam 8-track tape machine onstage under a spotlight and announced it as the fourth member of the band! The Reels, joined by a reel-to-reel. I don't know if everybody got the joke.

Their live show was quite an experience.

I mixed down the instruments we needed from the 24-track master tape and the band played along live with the 8-track. The drums, vocals and some of the keyboards were live, but anything else could be live or off tape. It was very difficult. I had to balance the mix depending on what the band threw at me on the night, and everything was worked out at the last minute. Dave would stand behind a screen playing his harmonica, the audience watching his silhouette, then he'd walk out and show that his hands were, in fact, empty! Another night he would play it live. It was mixing in the dark.

Dave got sick of the music industry screwing the band over and went into floristry for a while. That made me laugh. There he was, walking among flowers in the video for 'This Guy's in Love (with You)' and next thing he was a florist.

T.C.

By 1982 Models were Sean Kelly, Andrew Duffield, James Freud, John Rowell and Graham Scott. I didn't know much about the band outside of the studio. At the start of the year Mark Ferrie had left and James joined.

I did some live work for them. The police jumped us while we were on tour in Queensland. We'd stopped at a music shop to buy drumsticks and noticed an unmarked car pull in behind us. As we took off it followed us all the way to the Gold Coast. We were smoking a joint backstage before the show when the cops came in. I got caught with it in my hand, of course. The dumb copper opened it up and shouted, 'It's green! It's green!' The filter had been made from a torn Serepax packet. Models' manager beckoned the cops aside for a word and that was it, the show went on. As we walked out at the end of the night the cops were standing by the till, waiting to collect.

Fucking bastards.

Models seemed happiest when they were in the studio making things up. That's when they did their best work. They were at their peak – their artistic peak, not their commercial peak, which was yet to come. We did some interesting demos at Richmond Recorders in the middle of the year. Creatively the band was coming from another direction entirely.

T.C.

Early in my career Australian music was considered amateur, inferior to big international names. I never viewed it that way and it wasn't until years later I saw that cultural cringe existed. Australian bands struggled, and many I worked with moved overseas: The Birthday Party, The Go-Betweens, Laughing Clowns.

There was nothing inferior about them at all!

Countdown didn't play much indie music. Molly wasn't a fan and liked his pop pure, but some bands did creep through. 'The worst group I've seen in the last five years,' that's what he said when he introduced Sacred Cowboys. Mark Ferrie had joined the band on guitar. They were my sort of scene, cowboy punk. Singer Garry Gray was a ripper, a real showman, leaping into the crowd with a live chainsaw and whatnot. I recorded their single 'Nothing Grows in Texas', which was co-written by Greg Perano from Hunters & Collectors.

LISTEN
'Nothing Grows in Texas'—Sacred Cowboys

I wasn't aware at the time, but a lot of the records I was working on were totally different from anything that was being done overseas. I believe that's because money wasn't the driving force, unlike the mainstream Australian music business where their mantra was, 'We've got to sell so many hundred thousand copies, blah blah blah'. The underground alternative scene viewed things differently. Making music wasn't just about financial success.

T.C.

I monitor loud, but not consistently. Maybe too loud but it hasn't done me harm, I'm going blind but I can still hear alright! I like to see the speaker cones physically moving and don't think you're hearing properly otherwise.

Yamaha NS-10 speakers were released in 1978 and started appearing in studios in the early 1980s. Larger facilities had them first, so Richmond Recorders would have been later. NS-10s are nearfield monitors and replaced Auratones as the industry standard – the speakers you had to have.

But they aren't everyone's cup of tea.

I have a love-hate relationship with them. I trust their sound, but they're not nice to listen to. Earlier versions had problems with excessive treble, so people would hang toilet paper over the tweeter speakers to dull the top end. That never bothered me, I must have got used to it. My woofer speakers aren't white anymore, they're a yellow colour. Over the years they've become stained by cigarette smoke! NS-10s are light in the bottom end so you have to drive them hard, but if they're sounding good, even at moderate levels, you know you have a great mix.

NS-10s are in nearly every studio, though there have been better speakers built since. Some people now prefer to use a number of different monitors to check their mixes, but I find that confusing – something might sound right on these, but not on those. Don't do it. When mixing you've got to make a decision and wear it.

T.C.

Richmond Recorders became a drop-in centre for musicians, people would come past at all hours. It's a wonder anything got done. I have to confess there was a sinister side to this as well, namely drugs. The studio was a good place to score.

Helmut Katterl was a partner who had been around the studio since early in the piece, and unforgettable because he was a nut. Helmut had got himself fucked up. He was constantly fumbling in his pockets – it's a symptom of speed psychosis, one of the drug's psychological effects. Late one night I was chatting to him, and as he checked through his pockets he dropped a hundred dollar note on the ground. I put my foot on it and sat talking for an hour, waiting for him to go so I could retrieve it. Sorry, Helmut, I owe you $100! Forget the interest though, I couldn't afford it.

After a while he disappeared and I never saw him again.

If there was a problem Tim Stobart was the person I went to. He was at the studio all the time and, to his credit, tried really hard. He made some big mistakes, but who doesn't? Tim had good intentions but just wasn't great at running a studio.

T.C.

That winter, my drug dealer went skiing and didn't tell his customers. How rude! I knocked on his door, and to my surprise the Russell Street drug squad opened.

'Come in, young man!' they beckoned.

There were four other sick-looking junkies lined up on the couch who'd done the same stupid thing. The police searched like buggery, and even had their hand on the loose piece of wood that concealed the dealer's stash, but for some reason it didn't move. He probably hadn't left any, not with us vultures hanging around. When the police failed to find anything they dragged me upstairs to the bedroom and gave me a thumping. I was shocked. I didn't know that sort of thing went on – I was a sheltered middle-class suburban junkie.

'It'll stop if you sign this,' the head copper said.

Fucking oath I'll sign! Unfortunately, it turned out I signed a confession I was dealing heroin.

I was more than a little put out. Had I been older and wiser I would never have signed anything the coppers put in front of me. Luckily Tim Stobart, bless his cotton socks, said, 'I know a lawyer who will fix this.' He was an older dude, with a brother who was a detective charged with beating a prisoner to death in the 1970s. It cost me $1000 just to go to his office, which was a lot of money back then.

I sat and he rang the Russell Street drug squad.

'You have beat a confession out of my client,' he started, 'and we're going to contest it in court.'

He hung up the phone and peered at me over his glasses.

'That stuff will kill you,' he warned.

Within seconds the phone rang. He picked it up, listened for a moment and replied, 'Thank you very much.'

That was it, the charges were dropped and I was most grateful.

Six months later I was walking along Chapel Street in Prahran with Jo and a head popped out of a car window. It was him, the copper who beat me.

'I'm gonna get you, Cohen,' he taunted. 'I'm gonna get you!'

I went as white as a sheet and bolted into Coles supermarket, out the back door and into the rear car park. Thankfully I never saw or heard from him again. I bet he's a bigwig in Victoria Police, if he's still there.

T.C.

I've always been fond of Jo. We are still friends, but were a volatile partnership. Speed affects people badly and it can turn them quite strange. If you're a bit paranoid or scatty, it multiplies that by a billion.

Jo became a handful. I should have stuck with her, but she needed help and I couldn't give it to her. I needed help just as much. So we left Elsternwick and Ian Davis, The Ferrets' old drummer, took over the lease. I'd never known anyone like Ian. He trashed every place he lived in! The landlord at the time, I think it was the guy who owned the newsagent downstairs, complained to Ian that the previous tenant had banged nails in the wall. Ian said to me, 'I'll fix him, I'll give him nails', and he did. He got huge nails and banged up sheets of newspaper all over the walls.

Ian wasn't the sort of person to take advice.

I remember one time he was keen to check out an 8-track tape recorder advertised in the *Trading Post*. It was located miles away so he asked me for a lift. I was driving Mum's little red Mazda at the time. We got to this flat and Ian looked around and saw a pulpit with a Bible on it and pictures of long-haired girls playing acoustic guitars. It set him right off, god-bothering was not Ian's thing. As punishment, some desperate characters went back and robbed the poor man. They broke in when he wasn't home, knew what they wanted and took it to Ian, who rewarded them with heroin. I wasn't very happy about that. I'd unwittingly been involved in casing the joint.

T.C.

In 1979 the Fairlight CMI synthesiser was released. It was one of the first digital gizmos and an Australian invention to boot! At that time, digital sampling technology was unheard of. The Series II followed three years later and Duncan McGuire from the band Ayers Rock bought one.

It cost an absolute fortune, as much as a house.

Duncan was working at Richmond Recorders, so we spent a lot of time together. After leaving Ayers Rock he had moved into studio work, producing INXS's first album in 1980. The Fairlight became Duncan's main instrument. He set it up in Stevie Dunstan's mansion on Grange Road, Toorak. Stevie had decked the house out with pyramid-shaped speakers in clear plastic boxes and we'd sit around all night marvelling at the Fairlight. With a pen attached to the monitor you could draw a waveform on the screen and it would play that sound! Another feature, 'Page R', was a prototype music sequencer. It was fascinating, but I started to see what was coming – people staring at screens. That didn't do a lot for me.

Duncan produced a single for Doug Parkinson entirely on the Fairlight, a cover of the 1960s song 'Eloise'. We transported the instrument to Albert Studios and started to record, but it sounded like shit. In the early days samples had only 8-bit depth, so the Fairlight slowly got replaced by real instruments and the single never came out. The Damned had a hit with the song a couple of years later.

T.C.

Ian Davis became well known for drugs. Even though I considered my-self a serious amphetamine user, the amount Ian was using ... goodness gracious me. I could never have afforded anything like it.

Ian was coarse and probably hard to like unless you knew him. I once knocked on his door to buy a bit of speed while he was in the middle of a big deal. Two huge bikies jumped out at me, one over six-foot tall, with a machete strapped to his leg.

My life flashed before my eyes.

'No, no, no, no!' Ian yelled. 'He's okay. He's a music mate of mine.'

I peeked inside to see a mountain of marijuana.

'Tony,' Ian announced, 'this is the Enforcer.'

I said hello to Mr Enforcer and apologised for coming to the door at the wrong time. Gee, the people you meet! It was an education, to put it mildly.

Ian was a very talented man, but he never wrote anything new. Instead, he kept rerecording the same songs over and over again – some people just shouldn't take speed. The truth is nobody should. I found a woman to look after me, as so many 'brave' men do. Josie, my first wife. She loved music and was always following bands around. We married in May 1983.

It was a bad idea.

Twentieth Century

(1983)

Don Walker is one of Australia's greatest ever songwriters. His ability to write a pop song, political song or whatever just blows me away. Don liked the records I'd worked on and wanted *Twentieth Century* to capture the energy and intensity of Cold Chisel playing flat chat live.

I was terrified to be asked to work with such legends.

The band invited me to a gig in Melbourne as a special guest. Standing at the side of the stage I was in awe, they were so good. I couldn't believe it, to be that close and to see so much energy being put into it. My try-out came at Richmond Recorders on 1 August 1983 with the single 'Hold Me Tight', a rude song about fucking that lasted about two minutes. It was not great but alright and I passed the audition.

Don wanted The Birthday Party approach – the sound of a band bashing it out rough and hard. Unfortunately Jimmy Barnes didn't feel the same way. He was looking toward the 1980s American sounds of his solo career, a slick LA production. That's a pretty big chasm.

T.C.

Twentieth Century wasn't going to be a pleasant album to make. Cold Chisel was in its death throes. Steve Prestwich had already left, and by the time I got to Sydney in September it was agreed, this would be their final album.

Jimmy had quit the band.

They put me up in a scungy hotel in Kings Cross. It was nice, I'd get up in the morning and there'd be bloodstains all down the corridor! I've got no problem with big egos like Jimmy. Lead singers – Nick Cave, Mark Seymour, Tex Perkins – have got to have that self-belief to do what they do. I couldn't get up onstage and make a goog of myself like that, no way. Some people misread it as arrogance, but it's not. It's an essential tool to front a successful musical unit. Jimmy was demanding and I don't blame him. I wasn't what he wanted. Don had brought in an outsider to do the job.

We recorded the rhythm tracks for *Twentieth Century* at the Capitol Theatre in Haymarket. The Capitol had hosted the first Australian performances of *Jesus Christ Superstar* back in 1972, with The Ferrets' Billy Miller and K.D. Firth. It was bizarre, there was a mobile recording truck parked outside and microphones all over the place. The room acoustics were difficult to control but it worked – we captured a live sound. Being onstage probably helped.

LISTEN
'Saturday Night' – Cold Chisel

The sound effects at the start of 'Saturday Night' are real. I know, because I was abused by several people the night they were recorded. Don lived in The Cross. He loved it and was friendly with a lot of locals. We walked down Darlinghurst Road on either side recording the ambience to portable Nagra reel-to-reel machines, keeping in sync to get a stereo effect. Don had a tiny pin microphone clipped to his shirt and me a big boom mic on a stick, so of course I became the target for the angry drug dealers. 'What the fuck do you think you're recording?' And if you've wondered, it was a Saturday night. Don was adamant.

T.C.

I got a flat with Josie in Kings Cross. Talk about letting kiddies loose in a lolly shop, it didn't end well. We had a one-bedroom dog box on

Elizabeth Street, really cheap and with a fantastic view of the harbour. One whole wall was a window that looked out at the Sydney Harbour Bridge. It was wonderful, I'd sit and watch the storms roll in. These days few can afford a view like that and I don't think the block of flats still exists. I remember parking wasn't much fun because there wasn't any. You had to try your luck on the street. My car got pinched a few times, but I'd always get it back.

No wonder, every part of it was broken.

I'd bought another red Mini and ran the poor thing into the ground. There was a microphone cable tied to the windscreen wipers which came in through the side windows, and every time it rained I'd steer with my knees and pull the cable. When the tail-lights stopped working on a trip back from Melbourne I bought a couple of torches, covered the beam with red cellophane and gaffer taped them to the back of the car. That went on for quite a while until someone told me I just needed to replace a fuse! I was never very practical. I lost a lot of torches, as you can imagine. If a car pulls up with torches stuck to the side, someone has to steal them whether they want them or not. It wouldn't be Kings Cross otherwise.

T.C.

Years later I was sitting at a cafe in West Berlin listening to music. *That sounds familiar*, I thought. After a while I realised they were playing *The Axeman's Jazz*. The recording of Beasts of Bourbon's debut album is legendary and happened so quickly I still don't quite know how it came about.

The whole record was completed in one day.

The Axeman's Jazz was recorded at Paradise Studios on Sunday, 30 October 1983. It was the first time I met Greg 'Tex' Perkins, Spencer P. Jones and Kim Salmon. Some of the best records are happy accidents! Paradise was owned by singer Billy Field, known for the song 'Bad Habits', and was a high-end luxury studio used by bands like Cold Chisel and INXS. It even had a hot tub, not that I saw it. I didn't see Billy Field either. Beasts of Bourbon's manager Roger Grierson arrived at midday and paid my fee, $100. Paradise Studios was located at 70 Judge Street, Woolloomooloo, just around the corner from Kings Cross. A tempting place for me. I ran down to The Cross, spent my money on ice creams and lollies, came back and off we went.

The album was an event, as recording should be. It was captured live to 2-track, which means I had to do the final mix at the same time as the band was playing. That's difficult. A band like Beasts of Bourbon were not going to play something three times. They'd get sick of it and their performance would go stale, but they knew they had to run through each song once for me before recording. I'd get the mix going, try to remember when to turn everything up, they'd play the song again and that was it.

LISTEN
'Psycho'—Beasts of Bourbon

'Psycho' is a cover, and the only song the band spent any time on. They listened to a record of Jack Kittel's version in the control room a couple of times beforehand to learn the chords. I'd never recorded an album this way – it was spectacular.

T.C.

Beasts of Bourbon were inspired at exactly the right time to record. You can hear it, the way they played together as a group is beautiful. Spencer, Kim, Boris, James and, of course, I have to concede, Tex is pretty bloody good too. Onya, Greg! Everyone was fucked up, but just at the right level of out-of-it-ness, if there is such a thing.

I cut up the original half-inch 2-track tape to sequence the album, there were never any other copies. It's such a good-sounding record to my ears for that reason, because it didn't go through the process of being transferred from one tape to another. Maybe only someone who knows a bit about recording would notice the difference.

It sounds fresh and loud, jumps right out at you.

When we left the studio, Spencer was so drunk they had to pick him up by the arms and legs and dump him in the car park. But that was pretty good going because there was only myself and the band – no hangers-on – and I think we went through a crate of beer and a couple of bottles of bourbon. All that was left for me to do was master the album, and Don Bartley at Studios 301 on Castlereagh Street was the man for that.

Don is a clever fellow. He had a few strange gimmicks like phase cancellation but never much equipment. Just some good equalisers, a bit of compression and that was it. He would explain what he was doing as he went and didn't act like a wanker. That makes a difference. I would have liked more time to work on the mixes, or any time at all, but I've never heard anyone complain. I'm probably the only poor bastard who can hear the mistakes I made. *The Axeman's Jazz* is a bit wrong, and that's part of the charm.

T.C.

The Cold Chisel sessions had become hard going – there were a lot of clashes. As far as Jimmy was concerned I wasn't the right person for the job. Don Walker was patient, but Jimmy won in the end.

I wasn't behaving myself, as Don pointed out.

'Oh, look at you today. Your eyes look like two piss-holes in the snow!'

I thought I was discreet, but Don always knew when I'd been up to no good. He's very observant and that's why he writes such good songs. Personalities like Jimmy are different and tend to create situations. In the end I got thrown off the record and fair enough, I'd shot myself in the foot using things I shouldn't. Mark Opitz completed the album. I had finished most of it except for the mixing, though I did mix some.

Twentieth Century came out pretty well. Working with the band was a strange experience and not really one that I enjoyed, but it was certainly interesting. I was glad to have had a bit of a look.

The Cohen family at Christmas, 1983. Left to right: Tony, Margaret Cohen, Martin Cohen and Phillip Cohen. Image courtesy of the Cohen family.

T.C.

Chris Bailey is one of the funniest buggers I ever worked with. He saw himself as a court jester. He was, and is, very good at it. Chris created a lovely atmosphere by making people laugh and I think that's beautiful.

But he's not just an entertainer, he's a great musical talent.

I was asked to record The Saints' album *A Little Madness to Be Free* due to my work with The Birthday Party. Chris was a fan of the band, as they were of The Saints. 'Ghost Ships' was recorded at Albert's Studio 2 and was just the usual session, a day or so to get the track down and another for overdubs. The mixing, however, was very difficult. Chris had arranged the song in three sections and the instrumentation kept getting bigger and bigger. It starts off acoustic, then the band comes in and finally, pandemonium with strings and brass.

LISTEN
'Ghost Ships' — The Saints

I enjoyed mixing songs in parts and editing them together. That's the way it was in those days. Look back to The Beatles' records, particularly when they edited from stereo to mono. Very strange. If I hear anything like that I can pick the edits clearly. They're so obvious – *chop*, then all of a sudden, *bang!* – and all this extra noise erupts. It makes me cringe, but most people don't notice unless they work in studios. Our ears become more attuned. The general public buying the records don't know, and couldn't give a shit. As long as the edit happens on the beat, few notice the sound has changed.

'Ghost Ships' took three days to mix.

Each section of the song sounds totally different – it was a day between one piece of tape and the next. The edits are frighteningly bad, but Chris was amused. He knew it wasn't technically perfect and thought that was great. We had a good rapport and a mutual respect for what each other could do, but we didn't see eye to eye on my fondness for substances. I wasn't in good shape. Apparently I went out for a hamburger and wasn't seen for two days! Sorry, Chris. I guess that's why it took three days to mix.

I noodled around with a few other tracks on *A Little Madness to Be Free* but was too out of it to finish the whole album. To me it didn't matter, I was pleased with 'Ghost Ships'. I'd spent all my energy on that.

T.C.

Dynamic Hepnotics' 'Soul Kind of Feeling' still sounds good today. Whenever I hear it on the radio I think, *Fuck, I can't believe I recorded that!* It seems like a lifetime ago. The recording was innocuous, it just happened. The band knew exactly what they wanted and I love working with people like that.

LISTEN
'Soul Kind of Feeling' – Dynamic Hepnotics

Highlights of a Dangerous Life

(1984)

Albert Studios banned me. I was recording Zulu Rattle, a punk rock band with Stu Spasm on guitar. They'd saved up for months to pay for their big night of abuse, or should I say recording, with huge amounts of heroin, speed and marijuana.

It was a foggy night and things got out of control.

Zulu Rattle had no real intention of making a single, they just kept recording until everyone collapsed. At about 3 a.m. someone lit a joint the size of a forearm in the control room. The fire alarm went off and then *bang!* there was an explosion. A panel blew off the wall and fire-retardant foam started pouring out. It looked like snow in the studio. A sign lit up, 'EVACUATE AREA, EVACUATE AREA', but nobody was fussed. We started brushing the foam off the desk and got back to work.

The control room door had been locked. I heard a noise outside, then suddenly *Wham-Crunch-Bang!* an axe came bursting through the door and glistening golden helmets appeared. It was the fire department, and they were not happy. The recording was great, but the only thing we got was a copy on cassette. It was our own fault. Instruments went missing and Albert's seized the master tapes in lieu. I didn't want to take the blame, so I stepped out of the line of fire.

Albert Studios had had enough of me. I was as out of control as the band, which wasn't looked upon well. As the producer you're expected to keep an eye on things. I was having enough trouble keeping an eye on the desk!

T.C.

I had five dollars in the bank.

I'm absolutely hopeless, I can't handle my own money or schedule so I asked Roger Grierson to manage me. I bet he regrets that. It didn't last long and I tortured the poor man.

Roger ran a small label called Green Records, whose bands included Tactics, Allniters and Beasts of Bourbon. Most of the work I did for him was with The Johnnys. They were one of my favourite bands, and fabulous in their early form. People think musicians are a serious bunch, but The Johnnys were the last band you'd call serious. They were a laugh from start to finish. Spencer Jones, Graham Hood and Billy Pommer Jr played the music they set out to, brilliantly. I don't know what you'd call it, punk country? They certainly looked the part, in cowboy hats and chaps. Even spurs got a look in. It may have been a gimmick, but the band were really serious about doing what they did well, which was to sing very funny songs. Masterpieces like 'No Excusin' My Boozin''.

T.C.

Sometimes you take bands to a slick, sterile studio to record and they're not comfortable. But put them in a grubby studio which is a little rough around the edges, and you often capture more excitement.

The Johnnys' 'My Buzzsaw Baby (Really Cut Me Up)' was recorded at ATA Studios in May with Steve Nieve, Elvis Costello's keyboard player. How he ended up there I'll never know, it's one of life's mysteries. The session was really straightforward – The Johnnys could rock a venue and were able to translate that into a recording. They understood how the studio worked, so there was never any stress capturing a good performance. The band would listen to a take and say, 'No, we can do better', then go and do it.

The Johnnys recording 'My Buzzsaw Baby' at ATA Studios, 1984.
Left to right: Tony, Spencer P. Jones, Billy Pommer Jr, Graham Hood and Steve Nieve.
Image courtesy of Billy Pommer Jr.

LISTEN
'My Buzzsaw Baby (Really Cut Me Up)'—The Johnnys

Steve suited The Johnnys because he understood their humour. He was a lot of fun, though I'm not sure he was treating the recording very seriously. He was having a party! Steve was partial to a white substance usually snorted up the nose and I never saw anybody consume so much in my life. He made sure everybody had fun and that created a good vibe, which made for a really good recording.

T.C.

If I wasn't fuelled up I wouldn't answer the door. I remember Roger coming to pick me up after I'd moved to Bondi and he was out the front banging, trying to get me to open up.

'Tony, I know you're in there. Please come to the studio.'

I wasn't going anywhere, I'd run out of drugs.

The Johnnys were keen and liked a bit of debauched drug action. They were good drinkers, too, if that's the correct way to put it. I was mixing the band live at the time. They were forever getting into trouble and Spencer was no help – he was never backward in coming forward. The Johnnys' shows got brilliantly out of control, the sort of thing you aim for without consciously aiming for it. A combination of booze and hard rockin' music.

What I remember most about the band is laughter. They were an acquired taste, but people who knocked The Johnnys didn't get their humour. Spencer would make me wear a bright green cowboy hat at the mixing desk, which was embarrassing. He'd worn it on the cover of 'I Think You're Cute'. At RSLs in New South Wales one could easily get a can thrown at them for looking like a dill. Thankfully, the cans were usually empty. I had that hat for years and finally cremated it, or gave it away. Dreadful thing.

T.C.

Like all musicians struggling along in those days, Paul Kelly was keen for some money. I recorded demos for him at Paradise Studios in August. He was trying to get a deal and had songs he wanted to record, just acoustic guitar and vocal, to play for Michael Gudinski or whoever. Paul had achieved some success with The Dots, but this was to launch himself. Paul Kelly, the brand.

I had a session booked with Allniters, the ten-piece ska band on Roger Grierson's label. Ska is tiring on your ears, especially in a small studio. Trying to separate all those brass instruments? Give me a break. So, at midnight I pulled a headache, stopped the session and when the band had left, Paul came out to do his thing.

He'd been hiding in the microphone cupboard!

The main song he recorded was 'Cool Hand Lukin' about weightlifter Dean Lukin. The Olympic Games had just finished and the Australian won a gold medal. Paul wrote a lovely song following the television commentary and wanted to get it down while it was current, but since we had the mics up we recorded a few others – about eight in total. On that demo were classic Paul Kelly songs, later rerecorded and very successful. Songs you know well. As for Allniters? Sorry, fellas, but it was for a good cause.

T.C.

'My Buzzsaw Baby (Really Cut Me Up)' got remixed for The Johnnys' album *Highlights of a Dangerous Life*. I'm a bit hazy on the details of that, other than Ross Wilson, of Daddy Cool and Mondo Rock, had started producing the band.

We had a huge disagreement.

Big names aren't always the best people for the job. Ross saw The Johnnys as a pop band, while I saw them as tough. The band were broke and didn't have a profile, so Spencer and the guys were happy for any sort of help, especially from someone like Ross. They probably thought being more commercial might sell some records, but it wasn't a match. Ross is musically brilliant and his way of producing is great, but it wasn't great for The Johnnys. Ross liked to add doo-wops and shoo-bops to songs, nice things that were the opposite of what the band were trying to achieve. The Johnnys wanted edge. Ross cleaned them up and their music lost something as a result, because the rawness was part of the beauty.

I wish the band had been able to record their album with less interference. I don't blame Ross for wanting to help. He knew The Johnnys were great, but it was a clash of musical tastes and styles. It would have been a better idea for me to produce the album, had I been a bit more together.

T.C.

We started recording *Highlights of a Dangerous Life* at Paradise Studios in October. It wasn't a happy session. I'd get stoned and fall asleep at the mixing desk. We shouldn't have been recording so close to Kings Cross.

It's funny how you kid yourself. When you're stoned you don't think anybody else can tell, you think you're as cool as a cucumber while you're dozing off. Ross was in tears, not so much over the record but because I don't think he liked seeing me killing myself. He is a very serious person and was totally anti my behaviour. Of course, I wasn't going to get paid until the record was finished, so I pawned the odd microphone. It's not something I'm proud of.

I went to a Kings Cross pawn shop, the dirtiest place on earth, and was grabbed by vice squad detectives. I was lucky. I told them I had to pawn the mic to buy a ticket back to Melbourne and the shop owner vouched for me.

'He's a good bloke,' he said. 'He always comes back to pick up his equipment.'

I feel sorry for what I did to Ross. He's genuine and I know that I deeply upset him. Still, The Johnnys came up with a record, somehow. Ross must have taken it away to mix elsewhere. I don't blame him, I was in a terrible state.

T.C.

I've been an actor. A friend of The Ferrets, George, was an extra in *Mad Max Beyond Thunderdome* and got me a day's work. It was quite an experience. I never saw myself on-screen, so I must have ended up on the cutting-room floor. But I was there, hanging onto the side of the Thunderdome cage.

Filming was in Homebush. They only wanted people with really long hair or really short hair. That's how director George Miller saw an apocalyptic city – people either had haircuts or they didn't. The set was in pieces, so the Thunderdome cage didn't look anything like it appears in the movie, there was scaffolding and cameras you don't see. There's so much trickery in cinema, the way they frame the shot, different camera angles. I didn't have a prime position so couldn't tell if it was Mel Gibson fighting or a stunt man. What stood out most to me was the filming process and the way the crew slots together.

Americans are amazed that in Australia it takes so few of us to do what takes them so many. Their unions are very strict, so if you're a cable-hauling dude, that's all you can do. In Australia we just get it done. I'm proud of that. Unfortunately, though, *Beyond Thunderdome* is a crap movie. It was a dumb idea to cast Tina Turner, but that's what happens when the American studio provides another half a million dollars to your budget.

T.C.

I've always liked Roger Grierson. Some didn't have time for him but I never found him offensive. He was a very patient man. Our arrangement ended badly, and none of it was his fault.

I was unmanageable. A desperate drug-taking lunatic.

By the end of 1984 I had reached the end of my tolerance of Sydney, or should I say of people tolerating me. It was nasty. I was staying at the Bernly Hotel at the back of The Cross, above the Manzil Room. My sheets were polka dotted with cigarette burns and I would use the sink as a dunny because it was too far to walk down the corridor to the toilets. I left and drove back to Melbourne in the Mini. I think I swapped it for drugs when I arrived.

Workbook art by Tony, 1984. Image courtesy of the Cohen family.

Dogs in Space

(1985)

Bob Nimmo was from Sydney. He was the son of a wealthy man and wanted to work in music, so his father bought him half of Richmond Recorders. There were big plans – Tim Stobart had set up a record pressing plant next door.

But the studio became a hook-up place for drugs.

It was sad. There'd be musicians sitting in the lounge room who had nothing to do with the session, just waiting for the man. Lobby Loyde's guitarist Andy Fordham had developed a terrible speed habit and would be there day in, day out. If he didn't have any money he'd wait until someone else scored, then ask for a bit. I called him Cosmic Andy. He had a fabulously unique way of speaking where every sentence had 'a'rooney' attached to the end of it. 'G'day, bud-a'rooney!' he'd say. 'Have you got any of the gear-a'rooney?'

You tend to develop your own language on drugs. No one was calling anything for what it really was.

T.C.

I knew Lobby well and would see him at the studio all the time. He was the best fun to be with. Lobby lived the rock 'n' roll life. He liked to party hard and he liked hard-sounding recordings. As a producer he had all my respect.

I worked with Lobby on X's *At Home with You* in March.

The X line-up at the time was Steve Lucas, Ian Rilen and Cathy Green. I first went to see the band live in St Kilda and man, the energy. My jaw was on the ground! *Why aren't there a thousand people crammed in here?* I thought. There was a crowd of about ten.

LISTEN
'Degenerate Boy' – X

Ian Rilen was one of my favourites, of anyone who I ever worked with or knew. Everything about him was real. He was an absolute wild man and lived life with no bullshit whatsoever. Ian had written Rose Tattoo's 'Bad Boy for Love' and was their bass player. Fuck, he hit those strings hard – he used a fifty cent coin as a plectrum! That impressed me immensely. He'd break a few strings, though.

I don't remember much about sessions for *At Home with You* and can't even picture them. I was pretty out of it. My health collapsed toward the end and Lobby finished the mix. He did a great job.

T.C.

I was on the dole and had twelve dollars in the bank. Wild Pumpkins at Midnight rang up and offered me a trip to Tasmania, so I thought: *Alright*. There were no drugs around, so I drank like a fish instead.

Wild Pumpkins at Midnight were Tasmanian hippy protest musicians. All acoustic, anti-nuclear lentil music. Apparently ASIO would check them out at gigs. What a joke. I'd love them to have a file on me, I'd be proud of that. Guitarist Michael Turner was the brains of the outfit – most bands have someone like him, a person who steers the ship.

I slept on the couch at their house.

It was a very hippy environment, with chicken shit all over the floor, which was dirt. I couldn't make out where the backyard ended and the house started. I woke one morning to find a chook sitting on the armrest, staring at me! What a horrible thing to see when you first open your eyes. I got up and they were everywhere, white chickens with paint on them to tell which was which.

Michael went to India for a while and got lost in the hills smoking dope. God bless him. He discovered you could walk through wild marijuana fields with your hands out, rub them together and form a ball of hash. They had a bit of trouble getting him back, which happens. There are probably still some Australian hippies wandering the hills of India.

T.C.

Bob Nimmo was found dead in the toilet upstairs at Richmond Recorders in October. From then on the fun and games were headed south. Poor Stevie Dunstan had vanished the year before in mysterious circumstances and was never seen again. A drug deal gone wrong, perhaps? Who knows. I made an effort to clean up, without much success. It was beginning to seem like drugs first, music second.

The Bad Seeds arrived in November for an Australian tour. The band were Nick, Mick, Barry Adamson, Blixa Bargeld and Thomas Wydler. Barry was the bass player from Magazine, Blixa the guitarist from Einstürzende Neubauten and Thomas the drummer from Die Haut. It was Blixa and Thomas's first time to Australia.

They found the country a little strange.

Blixa and Thomas lived in West Berlin, and by comparison Melbourne was a country town. St Kilda may have been weird, but Blixa was too much. Even I was shocked by him at first. *What the hell have we got here?* I thought. This tall, skinny fella with spiky hair, marching down Fitzroy Street dressed in black leather daks, with a bright red codpiece held on by chains. Imagine getting around like that! We established a good rapport, though I didn't understand him well. It was the first time I'd worked with anyone from a non-English-speaking country.

Blixa is a great guitarist and watching him was a treat. Before each session he would set up camp in the corner of the studio and it was

116

different every album. He'd plug in gizmo after gizmo, just like Rowland Howard, but more precise. It's an interesting comparison, considering they both ended up with the same job. Rowland was abstract, he'd turn everything up and see what happened, whereas Blixa knew exactly what he was looking for. He took the blades off a small handheld fan and played the guitar with the motor shaft whizzing around on the strings. I'd never seen anything like it.

T.C.

We began recording *Kicking against the Pricks* at AAV in December. The studio had installed a new computerised Solid State Logic mixing desk in Studio 1, the SSL 6000E. It cost $350,000! When I pressed the wrong buttons the computer called me a fuckwit.

I must say I didn't feel 'in there' with the band on that album. It had been almost four years since I'd worked with Nick and Mick on *Junkyard*. After The Birthday Party, Nick had formed The Bad Seeds and recorded two albums, *From Her to Eternity* and *The Firstborn Is Dead*, with the English producer Mark Ellis, known professionally as Flood. He's a lovely guy and a very talented man.

I always thought his work might be better than mine.

Kicking against the Pricks is an album of covers related to Nick's influences, with songs originally performed by artists including Johnny Cash, John Lee Hooker, The Velvet Underground, The Seekers and even one by Tom Jones.

LISTEN
'Sleeping Annaleah' — Nick Cave and the Bad Seeds

I like recording pianos, but it's a difficult instrument to capture. Grand pianos are tough, upright pianos even more so. I open them up and get the microphone in close by removing as much of the cabinet as possible. On *Kicking against the Pricks* we used an upright with drawing pins in the hammers, which you can hear on 'Sleeping Annaleah'. The sound bit, it really jumped out.

T.C.

In January we moved to Richmond Recorders and Barry, Blixa and Thomas went home. Nick experimented and became much better at microphone technique. He'd started to realise he didn't have to scream, shout and bang people over the head all the time.

Some people have a good voice but they don't know anything about singing into a microphone and make a terrible mess of it. You want to be able to hear every expression. Nick became very thoughtful about how to get his voice sounding good and would sometimes get up close to intentionally distort the microphone, so that the imperfections gave punch to the words he wanted. We ended up recording enough material for a double album.

A lot didn't make the cut.

Kicking against the Pricks' inner sleeve says 'TIME & MONEY WASTED AT RICHMOND RECORDERS'. I don't remember the finer details, but it seemed Tim Stobart had taken advantage of the fact he was dealing with a record company and charged the band for days they didn't use. It was poor form, not to mention stupid, because The Bad Seeds never worked at the studio again. Mick was very angry – he kept a tight handle on the band for a long time, when he had to.

T.C.

I'd watch Michael Hutchence on *Countdown* and assume he was full of himself, so it came as a surprise to discover he was the total opposite. Michael didn't have tickets on himself. He was one of the most humble, down-to-earth people I ever met.

I got involved in Richard Lowenstein's film *Dogs in Space* because I worked at Richmond Recorders and had gained a reputation for achieving certain sounds. The film was re-creating Sam Sejavka's band The Ears,

118

who Chris Thompson and I had recorded back in 1981. Ollie Olsen from The Young Charlatans and Whirlywirld was put in charge of the music.

A few friends appeared in the film.

John Murphy was the drummer in Whirlywirld and had a small part as a heavy. It was funny because in person he was nothing like that, but he did have a rough-looking head so I guess Richard thought: *Great, he'll do!* All credit to Richard, being a director is a big job. There's no way I could control so many people – I was one of the hundred faces in the crowd outside the MCG queuing up for David Bowie concert tickets at the start of the film. I never managed to spot myself, so must've been cut out … again!

We began recording the music for the film in February. I remember that because Michael said it was an honour to be working with me. I'm sure I should have been the one saying that to him. It turned out that he was a fan of the hard-sounding recordings I'd made at Richmond Recorders over the years. Funny, because the soundtrack to *Dogs in Space* was the last thing I recorded there. The studio was put into receivership in March.

LISTEN
'Rooms for the Memory' – Michael Hutchence

I had a good time working on *Dogs in Space* and got along famously with Ollie. He had a fantastic imagination and would end up producing records himself, like *MaxQ*, the album with Michael and John Murphy a few years later. That was no surprise. Ollie had a knack of hearing when things weren't working and knowing how to fix them. That's good production. It's all very well to know when things aren't working, but you need to know how to fix them.

T.C.

Big power poles have a tension rod holding them into the ground. Belt one with a piece of metal and you'll hear the sound of a lightsaber from *Star Wars*. If you slow down the growl of an elephant you'll hear a spaceship.

Roger Savage had worked on the recording of *Return of the Jedi* back in 1983 and set up Soundfirm in South Melbourne when he returned. It was a fake cinema with a screen at one end, mixing desk in the middle and empty space where there should have been seats. *Dogs in Space* was mixed there in Dolby Surround. It was a gas. I had a joystick control and whizzed Rowland's guitar round and round the cinema with reverbs panning out behind me. I don't know if any of it was used in the film, it would have driven the audience mad!

I hate others mixing songs I've recorded, it's wounding.

Nick Launay mixed 'Rooms for the Memory' at Townhouse Studios in London. His work was always good, but I would have treated the song differently. I was never a fan of gated reverbs, even though I used the effect myself. *Kicking against the Pricks* was also mixed in London, at Strongroom, a couple of months earlier by Flood. I wasn't thrilled he'd done it, but I was thrilled with the results. Flood's mixes were great and not what I would have done, which in hindsight probably made the album better. The most important thing is good results.

Your Funeral... My Trial

(1986)

If you're lucky enough to work with a group of musicians who look like they might go somewhere, stick with them. Work with the band live, and if you haven't got a lot of studio experience, be an assistant when they're recording.

If you're doing good work, recognition will come.

Eventually I went overseas with The Bad Seeds. I could have gone earlier, but I was too frightened. I didn't have the money or the guts to make the trip without a job at the other end. There was plenty of work coming in at Richmond Recorders so I stayed, which I'm glad I did because I learnt more. But I wanted to see what was going on outside of Australia and felt that I might have missed out, so when Mick Harvey called with a plane ticket to London to record *Your Funeral... My Trial*, I was there.

T.C.

Josie and I relocated in June. London scared the crap out of me at first. I felt like a fish out of water and depended on others for comfort. Initially, at least.

Richard Lowenstein did a wonderful thing for me. He had directed the film *White City* for The Who's Pete Townshend and asked if I could get an interview for a job at Pete's recording studio Grand Cru, which was a barge on the Thames. Unfortunately I didn't meet Pete but the head engineer instead, and he didn't want no bloody Aussie upstart at the studio. So I went to Sarm West Studios in Notting Hill, which was lush. It was an old church that had previously been Basing Street, Island Records' studio.

Led Zeppelin and Jethro Tull recorded there.

Studio 1 had huge rooms for drum sounds, while Studio 2 was much smaller. I remember hearing an interview with Jethro Tull's Ian Anderson about recording the album *Aqualung* at the studio. It was a brand-new complex at that time and Led Zeppelin were working on the album *IV* in Studio 1, while Jethro Tull were in Studio 2. Ian Anderson said he was really disappointed with the sound of *Aqualung*, and in spite of having all the latest equipment he thought it was a shit studio. I listened to the album sometime later with that in mind and he's right, it doesn't sound very good. It's still a good album, but the sound doesn't compare to Led Zeppelin's *IV*.

Sarm West was where Bob Marley had recorded. I was told by a Jamaican: 'That window up there, man, that's Bob Marley's bedroom.' It was where he crashed when he was working at the studio, so the space had become sacred. And fair enough.

I met a few people at Sarm. I got an autographed photo of Boy George for my cousin, who was in love with him. I met Suggs, the singer for Madness, and even saw Freddie Mercury, which was very exciting. He breezed past me in his shorty-shorts that left very little to the imagination. God bless him. I love *A Night at the Opera*, it's a great record. 'Death on Two Legs (Dedicated to …)', what a way to open an album! 'Do you feel like suicide? I think you should!' Freddie got stuck into whoever that song was about.

T.C.

Nick Cave is a genius, as has been proven, and didn't get many bad reviews. Some didn't understand him, but those who did had respect. When a guy gave him a bad review for *The Firstborn Is Dead*, Nick wasn't happy and wanted to get his point across.

So he wrote a song called 'Scum'.

Mute Records had built their first incarnation of a studio in an office on Harrow Road. Nick and I locked ourselves in and binged on speed. We were there for a few days, but it felt like half an hour. He recorded an obscene vocal for the song, which got worse and worse until we rolled out of the studio in hysterics. It was silly, but lots of fun. I took over recording from Flood on *Your Funeral... My Trial* in August at Strongroom. It was a good studio. I'd catch the train to London Bridge, then the underground to Old Street. Nick and I ran amok, which disjointed things somewhat but there was always an assistant engineer at hand to do the hard work.

Drugs were a subculture of naughtiness which Mick Harvey didn't belong to, ever. That's why he's so active. Mick played a number of instruments on *Your Funeral... My Trial*. Barry Adamson had left the band and Thomas hurt his arm, so Mick had to keep things together. Nick was very lucky to have him.

LISTEN
'Your Funeral, My Trial'
—Nick Cave and the Bad Seeds

Mick was in quality-control mode quite often. It was hard work for him but he knew what to do – by then he had learnt the recording process. *Your Funeral... My Trial* is a great album.

T.C.

Hellish stories of Aussies living in London are fair dinkum. I went through a bad patch like The Birthday Party had years before, though not as extreme. We were living in Croydon, South London, and the landlady was a nightmare.

Our flat was rank. It had six layers of carpet because instead of re-carpeting, she'd just put more carpet over the top. A stray cat lived there and all the tenants would feed her. She came in through the window and slept all the time so we called her Mogadon, after the sleeping pill. I spent a lot of time with Mick, he was a good friend. Dad would send me footy newsletters from Australia and Mick was always keen to hear the Collingwood results, which made me laugh. You wouldn't think he was the type! I know a lot of music people who like football – Billy Miller and Molly Meldrum are one-eyed Saints supporters through thick and thin. Wooden spoon after wooden spoon. Nick, however, probably couldn't name a football team.

In September I joined Crime & the City Solution as their live mixer for a short tour of Germany. I didn't think I was the best person for the job, but I was part of the gang. It was a clique and they liked to stick close.

'You'll be right,' Mick said. 'Think of all the places you'll see.'

I couldn't argue with that.

Crime & the City Solution was Simon Bonney, Bronwyn Adams, Rowland Howard, Harry Howard, Mick Harvey and Epic Soundtracks. We travelled around the country for a week in a fifteen-seat minibus with three of the seats removed to make room for guitars, amplifiers and luggage. And smelly shoes! Katy, Mick's girlfriend, did most of the driving and I would relieve her as we were the only two people with a licence. I'd look in the rear-vision mirror and think, *Fuck, I've got some of the most talented people I've met in my life relying on me not to crash.* I took that responsibility seriously.

T.C.

At the end of the month two new members joined The Bad Seeds for a European tour: Kid Congo Powers on guitar and Roland Wolf on piano. I flew to Düsseldorf and found my way to Bochum by train for the first show. The group had been rehearsing in Germany.

Each tour The Bad Seeds would rehearse a batch of songs, then choose a set. It would vary from gig to gig, but they had their favourites. At Bochum the setlist was: 'I'm Gonna Kill That Woman'; 'Train Long Suffering'; 'Your Funeral, My Trial'; 'She Fell Away'; 'Long Time Man'; 'Knockin' On Joe'; 'All Tomorrow's Parties'; 'Sad Waters'; 'From Her to Eternity'; 'The Singer'; 'By the Time I Get to Phoenix'; 'Stranger Than Kindness'; 'The Carnival Is Over' and 'Muddy Water'. Kid and Roland were nervous so it wasn't a fantastic show, but the crowd liked it.

We travelled across Germany to Norway, Denmark, Belgium, The Netherlands, France, Austria and back to England. The shows were good and some of them were great. I knew when Blixa's guitar parts were approaching and would turn his fader up so the sound leapt out. People loved that, it was just like listening to the record only ten times louder.

But when things went wrong I didn't know what to do.

Foldback is the sound the band hears through the speakers onstage. I could never understand how I was supposed to mix that from the front of house – you can't mix something you can't hear! I had a bad experience in Germany, or was it France? Wherever, there was a low frequency hum onstage that I couldn't hear from the back of the hall, but it was brought to my attention with abuse from the stage.

'You fucking idiot, Cohen!' shouted Nick. 'Don't you know what you're doing?'

The audience turned around and stared at me.

'Come up here and have a listen, you dill!' he added.

So I did.

I walked down the aisle in front of angry fans to find the floor tom was feeding back. It became a comedy act where Nick would arc up at me toward the end of a gig. The joke was on me, but it brought a certain level of notoriety. It was my couple of seconds of fame.

T.C.

Nick and I were always trying to score, it was important at the time. We were desperadoes, hanging around railway stations in Europe where dirty deeds are done. I think Nick enjoyed the experience – he certainly got a few songs out of it.

But some places you shouldn't buy drugs.

After the show in Utrecht we drove to Amsterdam and saw the red-light district. I couldn't believe my eyes: rows of shops with half-naked girls in the windows and sinister-looking men lurking in the dark. We had knives held at our throats! It was scary, but Nick managed to score a large amount of smack and we got shit-faced. The next morning we hired a minibus to drive to Paris and stopped by the French embassy to get our visas. Amsterdam looked completely different in the daytime and was very pretty.

It was a five- or six-hour drive to Paris. We drove through Belgium and made it to the French border, where we were lined up at customs. No one spoke English on their side and none of us spoke French. Nick was really stoned, nodding off against the wall, so the guards decided to search the minibus.

Three times.

Bags of leftover smack and a syringe were gaffer taped under one of the seats. A customs guard put his hand on the seat and I thought, *Oh no, here we go*, but he didn't find it. Instead, he produced a syringe lid from Nick's pocket. I tried to explain it was a fuse cover, which it could well have been. Back then syringes had a long plastic lid. Ultimately, it turned out the guards just wanted some free merchandise, so a box of T-shirts later, we were on our way.

We rolled up to Paris hours late. I walked into the venue in Montmartre and there were two small red speaker boxes, the size of a home stereo, on either side of the stage.

'The fucking PA's not here!' I shouted.

I was wrong – that was the PA. What a nightmare.

Red became the colour of that gig. French feminists were waiting for Nick out the back after the show. What a fierce lot! You don't want to argue with them. They went after him with broken bottles but he got away unscathed, of course. Some big roadies helped him into the minibus and we sped off to escape the riot. The record company took us to a restaurant where I ate snails and a pepper steak, washed down with a bottle of red.

I had the next day off in Paris with Mick and Katy. The atmosphere of the city was fantastic – Parisians running around with bread sticks under their arms. We visited Notre Dame, which was the most beautiful church I'd ever seen. The stone gargoyles were so handsome, I wish I'd had time to meet them all.

T.C.

We'd travel all day in grotty minibuses and arrive at venues dying of hunger. There'd be food and beer laid out, which didn't happen in Australia. Not everyday food either, but dishes like steak tartare – raw mincemeat!

'Has anybody got a match?'

Nick's a funny bugger and likes a joke, but timing is important. At the start of each show I would come out with the band and go to my position. The desk was set and I'd hope everything started as planned, which didn't happen often. Once I remember us getting lost trying to find the stage. We were marching along like an army and passed through a kitchen at the back of the venue. Someone sent us this way and that, when suddenly we found ourselves back in the kitchen again.

'Yeah, Spinal Tap! Rock 'n' roll! Rock 'n' roll!' I hooted.

Nick flashed me the dirtiest look. Oh well, it was memorable.

The final shows of the tour were in England. The band had finished and Nick had his after-show refreshment and was dozing off in the corner. This dude came in, dressed in tight black leather pants with a big cowboy hat on. And signature sunglasses.

He walked up to Nick and said, 'Hi, I'm Bono.'

Nick looked up at this dude and said, 'What? Fuck off!'

To my surprise Bono smiled and walked off. I think he was amused that Nick had the gall to tell him to fuck off.

I leant over to Nick. 'Why did you tell Bono to fuck off?'

'What?' he replied. 'The leather man? I thought he told me he had a boner!'

I have heard that Nick has discussed this with Bono and apparently it didn't happen. But it did. I was sitting right next to him.

To Nick's credit he would get up onstage no matter how sick he was. He'd use the pain of withdrawal as part of his performance. He wouldn't get up whacked, which was smart. Mumbling and falling about the stage wouldn't have been a great idea. Instead, he would wait until after the show. I respect that, but I could never understand it or show the same control. Having a habit, I couldn't wait to get the stuff into me.

T.C.

I went all over the world with Nick Cave and his mob. I saw beautiful places and got paid for it, which was cool. On the way to America we played in Reykjavik, Iceland. There were black rock mountains capped with snow and so much water. Bays, inlets and rivers. I half expected to see dudes with horned helmets and axes!

Before the show I wandered down to the venue for a look. It was very cold. The air was clean and crisp, and the streets were covered with ice. The shop windows – not that you could tell they were shops – were filled with pictures of Ronald Reagan and Mikhail Gorbachev. It was a week after the pair had met for the Reykjavik Summit. The venue itself was small and grotty. Beer was illegal as the government had decided it was too dangerous, but you could drink pure spirits – 99 per cent alcohol! The crowd, of course, got really drunk. We received a huge amount of money for the show because so few bands came to Iceland.

The flight from Reykjavik to New York was the best. It didn't depart until 7 p.m., so it was late at night when we passed over Greenland. The sky was clear and we flew so close to the North Pole that I could see the northern lights on the horizon. It was beautiful. Emerald green streaks of light, like fire leaping thousands of feet into the sky. Far below sat icebergs as big as continents, floating in the ocean. We flew over northern Canada, where I saw oil rigs miles from anywhere.

And then came the lights of New York City.

I could not believe my eyes. The Manhattan skyline spread out below, as far as the eye could see. It was huge, miles and miles of skyscrapers. I fell in love.

T.C.

The hotel television had forty channels to choose from. Two showed non-stop movies, so I watched *Aliens*. Others sold products twenty-four-hours a day – they would show a necklace, then a number for you to call to order it. Another two channels showed nothing but religion, mostly crazy evangelists. A few more showed non-stop news and weather, while another, only sport. There was a twenty-four-hour stockmarket report and a daytime station for cartoons. One of the channels showed dirty short films after midnight with ads for massage parlours. Remember, this was the 1980s, and Australia and the UK had nothing like it. Of course there was also MTV, a non-stop music channel which showed horrible bands and drove you mad.

Walking the streets of New York was entertainment itself.

If the city looked good from the air, on the ground it was even better. The shops never closed and everything appeared so good you wanted to buy it. In the morning a giant roar of traffic started. It sounded like every driver in the city was honking their horn. There were people jumping out of cars abusing each other and beggars asking if I had change. When I told them no they politely replied, 'Okay, have a nice day.'

1986 Nick Cave and the Bad Seeds US Tour

Peabody's Down Under, Cleveland, Tuesday 21 October

The Ritz, New York City, Thursday 23 October

Cabaret Metro, Chicago, Friday 24 October

First Avenue, Minneapolis, Sunday 26 October

I-Beam, San Francisco, Tuesday 28 October

Variety Arts Center, Los Angeles, Wednesday 29 October

Town Pump, Vancouver, Thursday 30 October

Aztlan Theater, Denver, Friday 31 October

St Andrews Hall, Detroit, Saturday 1 November

T.C.

Nick, Roland Wolf and I went to Alphabet City on the Lower East Side. It was a drugs supermarket located in vacant lots. You would put money in a bucket which went up the side of a building and came down with whatever drugs you wanted. Louie, the tour manager, had specifically told us not to go there.

We were in Tompkins Square Park, our meeting spot, when a Hispanic chap in a leather jacket set off to score for us. We followed him through the park but he was racing, so we were having a bit of trouble keeping up. Nick tapped him on the shoulder and said – well, nothing, because the guy turned around and produced a gun.

'Don't touch the fucking jacket!' he snarled.

I can't begin to tell you the amount of fear that came over me. It was the first time I'd seen a gun up close, and in the hands of somebody crazy enough to use it. This guy was loopy. 'Follow me!' he said.

Alphabet City was a predominantly black neighbourhood, so we stuck out like golf balls, three snivelling white guys trembling with fear. We couldn't keep up with this chap, which was just as well. Give that one a miss! It's funny to look back on now, but at the time it was a different story. Just seeing a gun makes you imagine what could have happened.

Or what did.

Nick went down a street to buy syringes. Back then people would put used fits in a packet and sell them to you, which is scary because AIDS was starting to take hold. We're lucky we're not dead. Anyway, I was following twenty yards behind Nick, when I saw him turn a corner and vanish.

Roland was lovely, but a very serious fellow, your deep-thinking German type. We returned to our meeting spot in the park and sat waiting until the sun went down. When Nick still hadn't shown, we started to freak out and went to find the others.

T.C.

Nick didn't arrive for sound check at The Ritz the next day. A few hours passed, everything was ready to go and we were still waiting. We were sitting in the band room depressed when a guy from a music paper came in. I had long hair and am a skinny sort of fellow, so I put on sunglasses and did an interview as Nick Cave.

The journalist greeted me warmly and started the interview. 'Where do you get your inspiration from?' he asked.

'What the fuck's it to you?' I replied.

This guy was from Sydney, so I didn't expect to fool him, but he was completely taken in. He got a little suspicious when the band couldn't contain themselves and started howling with laughter!

It didn't look like Nick was going to show so Mick and the tour manager started ringing hospitals and police stations, and finally discovered that he was in jail. A couple of cops had jumped out and arrested him when he'd tried to buy the syringes. The gig was cancelled. I sat on the steps of the venue at East 11th Street with Mick Harvey and a couple of others. Punks were arriving with their hair superglued, dressed in leather, chains and god knows what. They'd spent days getting ready, with hair the size of the Empire State Building.

'Sorry, guys, the show's not on,' Mick said. 'Nick's in jail.'

Some took it well, but others were not impressed. Those who'd spent forty-eight hours doing their hair were particularly pissed off.

Initially the police refused to tell us which jail Nick was in. It was a practice called 'turnstile justice' where they'd throw junkies in jail for two or three days, move them around to different precincts until they're hanging out, then kick them out on the street again with no charges. They figured it wasn't worth the effort because they were just going to go and score again anyway. Mick visited and took Nick some cigarettes and chocolates. He was locked up with twenty other junkies and had three packets of cigarettes, so sold them one at a time for fifty cents each.

When they finally let him out, our flights were changed and another gig was scheduled at The Ritz for the end of the tour. Things were grim by that stage and about four people turned up. It caused a lot of grief. I didn't know until later, but we had to get out of town quickly – apparently organised crime was running venues and New York was the show 'not to miss'. It cost the group a lot of money.

Der Himmel über Berlin

(1986)

The flight back to London via Reykjavik and Luxembourg was an adventure. We all went to the airport, but there were only two seats available on the flight, so Mick Harvey grabbed Blixa and me.

'You and you. Get on,' he said.

The rest came days later when they could get a flight.

Jerry Lee Lewis and the prime minister of Iceland were on the plane. We flew to Reykjavik, where we thought we could get a connecting flight to London, but no such luck. The next flight was Friday and fully booked, so we were stranded in Iceland. We got a taxi into town and took a double room. Blixa was the only one with money as I'd spent all mine on drugs in America. It was freezing outside but the hotel was nice and warm.

There was nothing to do. The days in November are short so it was dark most of the time. We had one television station, which came on at five in the afternoon and went until eight at night and was in Icelandic. In the morning we rang London for an update and were told to wait. Blixa is not the most talkative character, but I had a couple of books to pass the time. Finally we got a call to board a flight to Luxembourg at five o'clock the next morning.

The flight attendants were big *Fräuleins* with braided hair, terrifying Viking *Frau*. We sat in the last row of the plane and stole a bottle of wine. Blixa was shit-faced after sitting up drinking all night and tried to gaffer tape the emergency exit shut. We were banned from Icelandair.

T.C.

There's a photo of Nick Cave and Tracy Pew sitting shirtless in the sun in Nick's mum's backyard. I think Tracy even has his cowboy hat on. He's got the most perfect killer look on his face that says: *What the fuck do you want!* It's a great memory of him.

Tracy died on 7 November after an epileptic fit. It hit Nick and Mick hard. Tracy was a lovely man and we had a lot of good times together, even if they did generally involve getting up to monkey business. Tracy was a fun person. He was a big drinker and a drug user, but he was incredibly intelligent. Some might argue that throwing a brick through a shop window in London to steal a typewriter is not the behaviour of a smart guy, but it was the behaviour of a drunk guy.

When Tracy died he was back in Melbourne studying.

Drugs have a lasting effect. In the early days we had a great time, everything was wild and amazing. That madness is fun, but as you get older the fun fades away. Drugs no longer have the effect they once did and instead you're left with a habit. That's when things get nasty. Suddenly people can't perform, or do anything much at all, without taking drugs. You do it just to feel normal. That put a lot of stress on Mick, who was watching his friends slowly kill themselves.

When you're taking drugs to keep from being sick, it's time to reassess the situation. Josie had got herself a job at Mute Records. Lou Reed rang up one day to find out who was recording The Bad Seeds. He was preparing for his *New York* album and must have heard their version of The Velvet Underground's 'All Tomorrow's Parties' on *Kicking against the Pricks*.

'Does he use drugs?' Lou asked.

Mute owner Daniel Miller is completely honest, so his answer was yes. Lou was off the stuff by then and didn't want to be around any of that behaviour. Fair enough, though working with him would have been interesting.

T.C.

At the time, we believed it was drugs that made bizarre, creative ideas come out. I now think that has nothing to do with it. Drugs are not needed for your imagination and, if anything, they stop ideas getting through.

They certainly stop many of them coming to fruition.

These Immortal Souls were Rowland Howard, Genevieve McGuckin, Harry Howard and Epic Soundtracks. Rowland and Harry were great together, Genevieve was good too. She had kooky ideas! That's what was great about working with these people, they were coming from another direction entirely. These Immortal Souls had such a great imagination, the only thing wrong was drugs. If it hadn't been for that distraction, they would have been hugely influential in the wider world of music.

Our recording sessions were all over London. Many a time I'd roll up to the studio feeling shithouse and say, 'Fuck this, let's go and score.' At the end of the year I did some work with Rowland and Epic on an album for Jeremy Gluck called *I Knew Buffalo Bill*, with guests Nikki Sudden and Jeffrey Lee Pierce.

LISTEN
'Gallery Wharf'—Jeremy Gluck

January 1987 was one of the worst English winter months on record and our flat in Croydon got snowed in. I tried to ring Josie and found out she'd buggered off with a roadie. *I've fucking had you!* I thought, so I packed my bags and moved out. I left the landlady to her, figuring it was a fair trade. In truth, Josie did me a huge favour. After mixing live shows for Nikki and Rowland I moved to West Berlin, and the years I spent there were some of the best of my life.

T.C.

Heathrow Airport is really big. I was late for my flight, so had to run to the gate while the plane was held. My seat was at the back and everybody glared as I walked down the aisle. When I finally made it, there, in the window seat, was Mick Harvey.

'Oh no, not you!' he jeered.

West Berlin was a rich artistic place, full of creativity and passion. It was one of the city's selling points. Perhaps it was a backlash against the war? It's amazing the artists who were there at that time, including Crime & the City Solution and, of course, Nick Cave and the Bad Seeds. As an Ausländer I felt most welcome. Nick was a tourist attraction, which was bizarre. There were postcards of him sitting in his room under a painting of a woman with open legs.

It read: *Nick Cave, Berlin.*

Surrounded by East Germany, West Berlin was an 'island' of Western decadence in the middle of Soviet Europe, and having the Berlin Wall up was great, for us. It made it a cheap city to live. You could smuggle deutschmarks in your shoe and go to the east for amazing meals that would have cost thousands in the west. As for the east, they loved the western money coming in.

Mick had got himself an apartment, so I freeloaded off him. There are so many great stories to tell. It was a naughty time, but West Berlin was a naughty town. If you wanted mischief, it was the place to be.

T.C.

Friedrichstrasse is a train station in what was then East Berlin. You couldn't leave the station unless you had a visa or pass for the day, but you could get off onto the platform, buy duty-free cigarettes and booze, jump back on the train and three stops later be back at Kochstrasse station in the West. It was a great lurk.

Russian cigarettes aren't flash, but their vodka works!

My train stop was Görlitzer Bahnhof in Kreuzberg. I remember killing lots of time at Nick's place – he was living with Christoph Dreher at

Dresdener Strasse 11. Christoph was the guitarist in Die Haut, which translates to 'The Skin'. I spent most of the time sitting in Nick's room upstairs, dribbling and bothering him in the middle of the night. It was the first time I felt we got close. Maybe he enjoyed having one of his old Aussie mates around.

Nick was working on his debut novel, *And the Ass Saw the Angel*. He was obsessed. I watched him write for days on end, speeding through the night. He had a .45 handgun he'd play with, rolling it around his fingers. It was an unpleasant story he wrote and his ideas were disturbed. There were even pages scribbled in his own blood. He would bounce ideas off whoever was sitting around and hand me the odd sheet to read.

It was stunning.

I may have helped him with some Australian slang. In the end, though, he banned people coming into his room. He'd gone Tolkien and had grand plans for the work to be three volumes, with maps and histories. But all that got thrown out by the publishers and he ended up with a small book.

The music we recorded to accompany live readings was just Nick. It was very avant-garde, plucking pianos and things like that. Weird atmospheric noises. No real music, or what I call music – beats and melodies.

T.C.

I should have gone to West Berlin years before. It was full of great people and great recording studios. Hansa Tonstudio was the best I'd seen. It was right next to the Berlin Wall, at Köthener Strasse 38. We did so many brilliant recordings there.

Hansa had an amazing atmosphere. It was where David Bowie had recorded *"Heroes"*, though I don't think I was aware of that at the time. I was more taken by evidence of Nazis. I've always been interested in World War II history and it fascinates me that a race of people could be so badly misled.

I've got Jewish blood too.

Studio 2 at Hansa, the Meistersaal, was an old Nazi ballroom and

Hansa Tonstudio, 1987. Image by Michael Jödicke.

one of the few buildings in the area that hadn't been flattened in the war. The ballroom stood as it was in the 1940s, with a projector room up in the corner to show propaganda films of the Nazis' 'glorious victories'. In the attic was a mix room, with windows looking out at the Berlin Wall and guard towers opposite. Further down the road was Hitler's bunker, which no longer existed. I believe there's a concrete slab where the entrance used to be. It was intense – you wouldn't be human if you weren't a bit creeped out by the place.

T.C.

Once you've been taught something, it's very difficult to go against that knowledge. But that's the way it was for me, and my time in West Berlin helped. It marked a turning point in my life as an engineer and producer.

Studios weren't run like they were in Australia. It wasn't a business, everything was done purely on an artistic level. Some seemed to have no idea what gizmos they had or what they were meant to do, so totally misused them. They would patch things together and get brilliant results. It was perhaps too avant-garde for mainstream work, but I couldn't help but be impressed. What it taught me to do was to tear up the rule book completely. At Hansa I did whatever I wanted and it was a joy. The assistant engineers were so efficient that before I could want anything, there were three people there to do it for me.

'Oh, you want to do this?' they'd say. 'Ha, you are crazy! Magnificent, we love it!'

I'd never had that support before.

Studio 2 at Hansa was massive, the size of a church with a stage at one end and mobile screens to control the acoustics. Every surface was wood, so the sound was magic. The control room, though, was very rough. The monitors were up on milk crates, if I remember correctly, and equipment was held together with crocodile clips and gaffer tape. By contrast, the mix room in the attic was very slick, with a pristine state-of-the-art SSL console. You couldn't want for more – they were two completely different worlds, which together made for beautiful records.

T.C.

German microphones are the best – Neumann and Sennheiser. AKG are good, too, but they're from Vienna. The Neumann factory was on Charlottenstrasse, just near Checkpoint Charlie. When I caught the train to work it travelled right past and I would bow down in respect.

The most fun I had at Hansa was recording 'From Her to Eternity' for the Wim Wenders film *Der Himmel über Berlin*, which translates to *Wings of Desire*. Meeting Wim was wonderfully strange. We all gathered at his office so he could explain to us his ideas for the movie. He started talking away, telling us about the scene with Nick performing 'From Her to Eternity' with an angel standing behind him, and then suddenly stopped, almost mid-sentence.

We looked at each other.

Some time passed. Then, just as suddenly, Wim said, 'Ah ... what was I saying?'

'You were telling us about the angel,' we replied.

'Yeah, yeah,' he said, and on he went. This happened a few times, so we became accustomed to it. Imagine a guy directing a huge movie who completely loses the plot? Fascinating.

Wim wanted 'From Her to Eternity' to sound like the band playing live, so I put a whopping great PA in Hansa and we rerecorded the song. It sounds like it's blasting out of a PA because that's exactly what happened. I kept playing the mix back at me and rerecording it, but what I could have done in an hour I spent all night doing! You don't get to muck around with a double 4-way PA in a huge room every day.

The band scene was filmed at the Hotel Esplanade on Potsdamer Platz, right near the Wall. The building isn't there anymore, and even then it was bombed out. The live recording from Hansa is what the band mimes to in the film. I was in that scene but must have got cut, bloody tragic. That makes it a third time!

LISTEN
'From Her to Eternity' (1987)
—Nick Cave and the Bad Seeds

I did really well out of that job. I got paid two hundred deutschmarks a day, which was close to two hundred Australian dollars back then, just to press play. They'd shout, 'Roll sound!' I'd start the tape recorder and that was it. You can guess what happened to the money.

T.C.

West German cops wore lime green, ill-fitting uniforms. I think that's because they didn't want to look like Nazis. They certainly didn't look like cops, more like clowns! Still, I've got a lot of respect for them. They don't fuck around with things that are not worth fucking around with.

Nick was away and I was staying at his place. I was off my face and decided I wanted a bottle of booze. I couldn't speak German, so mostly shopped in supermarkets where I didn't have to converse with anyone.

The only thing I can remember is trying to stuff a bottle of whisky down my pants with two cops standing in front of me shaking their heads! They hauled me away and I got stuck in a tank with twenty German drunks. I have no idea how long I was there. I was so out of it I slept for a day or two, then a cop appeared at the door calling my name.

'Mr Cohen, your case has been heard.'

My case? They obviously hadn't bothered waking me for it.

'Kangaroo court!' I roared. 'This is outrageous!'

'Just go,' the cop said wearily, opening the door – it's best not to bother with idiots.

I stepped out of the police station somewhere in West Berlin. I had no idea where I was or how to find my way back, so I went to a train station and kept reading names until I found one that I knew. When I returned to Nick's place everything was as I'd left it, including my drugs and spoon, so I picked up from where I'd left off. I did learn some lesson, and didn't go shoplifting again.

Tender Prey

(1987)

West Berlin had bars for poets, bars for painters and bars for musicians. That's how it was. You'd go to a different bar depending on your interests. In reality, though, they were just places to get pissed. The Ex'n'Pop in Schöneberg was for musicians, particularly Aussies. We'd all hang out there.

The locals found us very odd.

I'd get free drinks and was popular with the girls, which didn't bother me at all. I met up with a crazy American named Claudia. She had purple hair and rode a skateboard all over the city – quite ahead of her time. Claudia was the black sheep of her family and had a rich father with a financial company in London, who I never met. She put me up in a squat at Gleditschstrasse 11 called The Ruin.

The building was bomb-damaged on the outside, but inside it was luxury, except in winter when the pipes froze. That was a bit of a drag. You had to get buckets of water to flush the dunny! The Winterfeldtplatz opposite iced over and people would skate on it, then from spring it operated as a Sunday market. Around the corner was Café M where all the musicians went. They gave you food and coffee just for being part of the scene, it didn't matter if you had money. That wouldn't happen these days.

I lived at The Ruin for quite a while. Band demo tapes started to appear, which was a good sign. Mick Harvey was always trying to get me work. I recorded *Headless Body in Topless Bar* for Die Haut at Hansa in May. Nick Cave, Anita Lane, Kid Congo and Mick appeared as guests. That was bizarre. I sat in the control room while the band talked among themselves and after a while they turned to me and said, 'Okay, Tony, now we do it.'

'Do what?' I replied.

'Ah yes, sorry,' they said. 'We forget you don't speak German!'

Communication is important when recording, but it's not always easy. Particularly when you don't speak the same language.

T.C.

The Ex'n'Pop would open at 9 p.m. and shut when the last person left. Simon Bonney and I worked there as barmen for a while, which was funny. Two Aussies pouring beer the wrong way and getting into trouble. I remember working until around midday. We'd finally get all the drunks out, us included, close up and stagger home, lucky to be alive.

The bar was run by Evelyn, whose boyfriend, Harry, was a poet. He was most interested in Australians and our strange ways, particularly the use of slang.

'Fucking starve the lizards!' I'd exclaim.

'Why do you not want to feed the lizards, Tony?' asked Harry.

'No, no, it's an expression,' I replied. 'It means "good grief".'

'Oh, Tony, you must tell me more …'

Harry loved turns of phrase about pissing, like 'Point Percy at the porcelain', and hearing old-fashioned gay slurs that were common at the time. We don't say those things now, they're offensive, but back then there were people at the bar with notebooks writing this rubbish down. I remember sitting up the back of a club listening to him give one of his poetry readings. It was in German so I couldn't understand a word he was saying, then all of a sudden I hear, '. . . and the shirt-lifters! And the pillow biters!' Who knows what his poem was actually about.

God bless you, Harry, I hope you're still alive.

Simon and I worked at the Ex'n'Pop on and off for about six months, until we got the sack for short-changing the till for other pursuits. It wasn't personal. We had a problem that required money, so occasionally we dropped a 100-mark note down our socks. I felt bad and gave Evelyn my vinyl collection, which was copies of albums I'd recorded. I could only pay her with what I had, and that was it.

T.C.

Blixa's lounge room had one big easy chair and two speakers. If you came to visit you had to sit on the floor! He was obsessed with ice for his vodka and if there was none backstage he'd spit the dummy and carry on like a prima donna, so the band bought him an ice-making machine for Christmas as a joke. It made a horrendous noise.

Blixa loved it and didn't get the joke at all.

Einstürzende Neubauten were fantastic. They played the Tempodrom in June, a big circus tent in Tiergarten. It was scary. The band were chain-sawing through sheet metal with sparks flying everywhere and hair catching on fire. It could only happen in West Berlin back then. Afterwards we walked home via the Reichstag and Brandenburg Gate, where just a couple of weeks earlier Ronald Reagan had given his 'Tear down this wall!' speech. He had come to celebrate the 750th birthday of Berlin, which was bizarre given that was a date the Nazis had made up.

I wonder if Ronnie knew about the riots his visit sparked? A car got set on fire right outside our front door. It was a hoot. I was looking out the window and saw all these people run past, then to my amazement riot police with helmets, shields, clubs and water cannons chasing after them.

T.C.

In July I started work on demos for the Crime & the City Solution album *Shine*. Simon and Bronwyn Adams had been thrown out of their flat, so we put them up in our spare room. They brought a television with them but it was useless.

All the shows were in German!

Crime & the City Solution was Simon's band. They had started back in Australia at the same time as The Boys Next Door with a different line-up, but I only vaguely knew of them then. Simon had a heart as big as they get. He was a unique artist, and so was Bronwyn, who co-wrote the lyrics. Mick saw something in the band that no one else had, and he was spot-on. Simon had a very strange way of working. The band didn't know what to play to his vocal, so we would record him singing with a click track and then work out the musical accompaniment later.

LISTEN
'Home Is Far from Here'—Crime & the City Solution

Mick was passionate about that band, it was his joy. He loved to be creating music from something so abstract. As I saw it, The Bad Seeds were becoming more his bread and butter. He had less control of them as time went on, especially with a man like Blixa in the band, who is a law unto himself.

T.C.

Nick was wild. He took the reins and got a manager, Jeanette, who arranged phoney student cards for us to get travel discounts. We went on a few short tours throughout the year and got up to all sorts of mischief in Athens.

Anyone who had English pounds in Greece was a millionaire.

There had been a deadly heatwave in the city that summer and old people were dying everywhere. We turned up and stayed in a hotel with air-conditioned marble rooms. It was the first time we lived like royalty. At the shows I met two girls. One couldn't wait to get me back to the hotel, but I chose the other and she took me to her mother's place! It was a good experience, but not quite what I was expecting. I sat down to a Greek family dinner with mama, grandma and the whole family, and then slept in another room.

I stayed on in Athens for a couple of days because the drugs were so good.

T.C.

The first session for The Bad Seeds' album *Tender Prey* was at Hansa on Monday, 7 September. I got paid three hundred deutschmarks a day and spent a third of it on drugs. We were really hitting it, especially the speed, which was a motherfucker.

Things got blurry.

The control room at Hansa was out the back, three hundred miles from the recording studio. You had to walk down corridors to get there. In the control room there was a small black-and-white monitor hooked up to a camera to see what was going on in the ballroom. It captured Nick and me wandering out of the studio with a tape recorder under our arms! Someone called us about it the next day.

'Why did you take the tape recorder?' they asked.

We made up some story about experimenting at home.

'Okay, just bring it back.' So we went to the pawn shop and retrieved the tape recorder.

It was a manic time, we were working long days and very rarely sleeping. Flood added some overdubs to the album later that month in London but we didn't consult with each other, Mick knew what he wanted done.

T.C.

Nick and I stayed in Christoph Dreher's flat while he was out of the country. Christoph was really straight, so was probably horrified at what he found when he returned. We weren't houseproud.

Nick liked to push the envelope in all parts of life, and driving was no different. He didn't have a licence. I remember being a passenger when he got pulled over by police, so I handed him my licence. At the time, Australian driving licences didn't have photos, so he was Tony and I was Nick. The cops were a bit astounded to see a licence without a photo on it, but everything was going well thanks to the language barrier.

'That's how it is in Australia,' we explained.

Next thing, a friend passed on a pushbike and yelled out, 'Hi Nick,' and turned to me, 'Hi Tony.' The coppers looked at each other, then looked at us. They knew they were being had, but we were too much trouble. *Fuck these idiots*, they thought and sent us on our way.

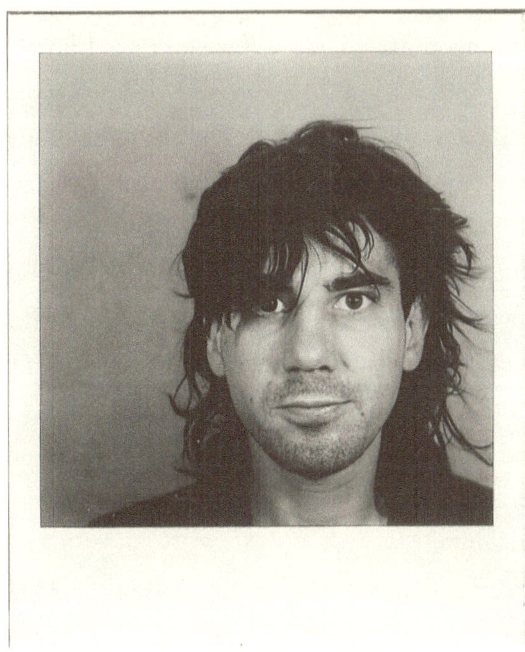

Tony in Berlin, 1987.

We had two lesbian drug dealers we would meet. One dressed in butch overalls and the other was a gorgeous Spanish girl with long curly black hair. Overalls – the boss – had a small rubbish bin covered with pictures of Nick Cave. If she was in a bad mood she'd make us wait in the park for hours, hanging out in the freezing cold. I suppose she thought it was cool to have something over the great Nick Cave. He was 'Sunday's Slave'.

T.C.

Talk about punks, what a pack of wimps.

I was working in the mix room at Hansa and heard two shots, *Bang! Bang!* I squinted out the window at lights and sirens, and saw the head and arms of a dead East German guard hanging over the Berlin Wall. His mates had shot him trying to escape to the West. It put things in perspective – I called off the session and went home.

I started mixing *Shine* in December.

I've got a strange, scrambled way of working. I know how to use most pieces of equipment, but I don't necessarily know what they do, or why they do it. That works for me, but I'm not recommending it. Find your own way of working. Be unique, you'll hear if what you're doing sounds good.

The SSL console at Hansa was slick and clinical. I had the luxury of noise gates on every channel to get rid of hiss and buzz, instead of having to manually switch instruments on and off. Alex Hacke from Einstürzende Neubauten had replaced Rowland Howard in the band. I'd listen to his guitar parts and think, *Fuck, that is so clever*. He came up with ideas I didn't expect. They are the artists you care about working with, that really mean something.

The Crime & the City Solution sessions were a joy. Mick had everything under control, and that's him at his best. It's a shame Simon had other ideas. He decided to move to America a couple of years later and give the band a miss. I think that would have hurt Mick. He'd put in a lot of time and effort.

T.C.

Nick recorded more vocals on *Tender Prey* at Vielklang in the middle of December. It was a small demo studio with egg cartons on the walls and mattresses over the windows, held together with sticky tape and god knows what.

I've always liked shabby, slapped-together places.

Vielklang was next to the Berlin Wall, which went right down the middle of the street, splitting it in two. We would leave the front doors open just to see the Wall. That's where 'Deanna' was recorded, which was a loose idea Nick had for a song. He fiddled around with a Hammond organ while Mick hit a floor tom. It wasn't meant for the record but we ended up using it – drums were recorded over the top and the track grew, with bits added in London and more back in Australia.

As you can tell, *Tender Prey* wasn't a coherent, continuous session. It would crop up for a week here and there, which is part of what makes the album unique. It's a product of an out-of-it feeling. It must have been difficult for Mick. He's quite an organised person and was watching a complete ratbag situation going on around him. I don't know how he put up with it.

T.C.

I returned to Australia in February 1988 with enough drugs to make it through the flight. I was rowdy, carrying on and annoying everyone. When the plane came in to land I awoke and was covered in cigarette butts and ash.

Things weren't so funny then.

I raced to the toilet to get rid of any drugs I still had. They broke down the door and questioned me at customs for hours. When I finally gave up the name of a dealer that didn't exist, they let me go. My dear parents had been waiting outside for me the whole time. How sad. Nick and the band were flying over for a short tour, so I rang to let him know about the trouble.

The band arrived in Melbourne and Roger Grierson booked them into a cheap beach-house motel in St Kilda. We were sitting outside on the balcony when a chap with a briefcase came in the front gate – it was Roger.

Blixa leant over the balcony. 'Are you the tour manager?'

'Yes, I'm Roger.'

'Good. Get me some speed!' Blixa demanded.

'Sorry. I don't buy drugs for bands.'

'Then you are not the tour manager,' Blixa declared. 'You are just another arsehole.'

Those two became great mates, as you can imagine!

Blixa and Thomas struggled with the Australian heat at that time of the year, they'd never experienced anything like it. In Adelaide it was so hot the road was melting. We were staying in a hotel with no air conditioning, dying from the heat, so would walk up the street every ten minutes to buy more ice-cream. Thomas was falling to pieces. Blixa decided to quit at some stage, he got shirty and said he was going home, but they managed to talk him out of it.

T.C.

The Ferrets' Ian Davis was one of the great characters that ever lived, but he burnt out quickly. I caught up with him when I came back to Melbourne. Ian had started making amphetamines and testing it on himself. You can hear him sing backing vocals with Mick Harvey on 'Slowly Goes the Night'.

LISTEN
'Slowly Goes the Night'
—Nick Cave and the Bad Seeds

Ian had become totally paranoid. He'd boarded up the windows of his house, dotted microphones about and would sit in a dark room listening to everything that went on outside. There might have even been cameras. He had been diagnosed with a spinal problem and his bones were dissolving. That's what speed does, it leaches calcium from your body. I went to visit him and saw his pushbike outside, so I knew he was home. I knocked on the door and called out, 'Ian, it's Tony. I don't want anything, I just came to say hello.' I went up the street to buy some smokes, came back and his pushbike was gone.

I never saw Ian again. The drugs killed him.

Everything had to stop. Nick and I were so sick that sessions at Record Plant Recordings were starting six hours late because we hadn't scored. I got more of the blame for the situation than I deserved, but that's my opinion. *Tender Prey* was the end of me for a while. I didn't want to be involved in music anymore – I'd lost interest.

I took a long holiday.

The Low Road

(1988)

'I wish I'd never helped you get that job,' Dad said.

What can I say? I'm a product of my era, and in the 1970s everything was going. Drugs were cheap, easy to get and most of the people I worked with were involved in one way or another. Booze was a constant, of course, because it's legal. I did my health some terrible mischief, but shit happens. If I was going to do that, I was going to do that, and so be it.

I'm still here and got a few marbles left, so I'm doing alright.

I returned to Australia in September 1988. It's a foggy part of life, I didn't know where I was or what was happening. Mum and Dad had bought a small 5-acre farm in South Gippsland. What a shock! From West Berlin and London to Kongwak, population one hundred. I'd still like to live there. It was therapeutic being in the country, relaxing away from the pressure of it all. There wasn't much to do, so I stayed on the farm drying out. I watched a bit of cricket, Australia versus the West Indies. A green picture on the television is good to doze off to. I was in such bad condition, it would take me a few years to get my strength back.

T.C.

I first got on methadone when I moved to Kongwak. A government program had been introduced in Victoria in 1985, and three years later there were a few hundred patients. It took a long time to get in, so I was really hanging out.

I'm a strange case. Most people stop withdrawing after a couple of weeks, but I'd go for a month and still be feeling sick. I don't know what was wrong with me, maybe it was psychological? Finally, I was enrolled for treatment at a clinic in the city.

It was horrible, and so were the staff.

I got dragged in, stuck on a bed and jabbed full of 'antidope', some drug that made you withdraw. Then everyone stood around observing my symptoms. Twenty young medical students came parading through. 'Oh yes, look – he's got goose flesh all over him.' It was torture. I was told that the pain would wear off, but it didn't. Luckily I had a pocket full of codeine tablets or I would have been in big trouble.

At the end, I got a methadone prescription for the chemist in Wonthaggi. The first day I took the stuff I was blissed. Oh man, the relief was uncanny – they must give you a really big dose to get it into your system. Driving back to the farm I started nodding off, so Mum had to take the wheel. I thought, *Jesus, this is going to be good.* But it never happened again. I got stoned for one day and that was it.

What a disappointment.

T.C.

Germans have always been good at pharmaceuticals. It was said that methadone was invented by Hitler's scientists during World War II, but I don't know if that's true. The story goes that many of his top generals were addicted to opium and when the Allies surrounded Germany they couldn't get their drugs in, so he got his scientists to invent a synthetic.

That was adolphine, later called methadone.

It's a prick of a drug – makes your bones weak and your teeth fall out. Hitler's revenge! Some people also gave that nickname to the Volkswagen, but I found them to be good cars. The little beetles were great. My Kombi van? Not so much.

Once a month I'd drive to the clinic in Melbourne. I hated it and was against the whole thing. I wasn't against taking methadone, but the clinic's ideas for treating addicts were wrong. Paint pictures? Group therapy? I wouldn't have a bar of it. Looking back, it was my fault for going to a government facility, but I didn't know private doctors were treating people like me. Things are better these days, but methadone is still 'liquid handcuffs'. You're stuck in a cycle of doctors and chemists.

Thankfully most people I know managed to get off heroin. A few didn't get the message, but take it from me: your work suffers for it, and your health suffers really badly for it.

T.C.

The fall of Richmond Recorders is an interesting saga, but sad. It was a successful independent studio where many great records were made. Tim Stobart ended up in court for years and was working in film, doing lighting, when everything came to a sticky end.

He was sent to jail for a few months.

By the time I left the studio, Chris Thompson had moved in as engineer. They were dark times for Chris, but fortunately he fixed himself up and did well. The band Painters and Dockers bought the studio, with Lobby Loyde running the record-pressing plant next door. As far as I know the cops got very interested in the place. Tax problems? Dodgy dealings? Whatever it was, the studio came to an end and the receivers arrived in early 1989. Chris saw the place getting auctioned off and it broke his heart. Apparently he was very disruptive. 'No, you can't sell that! You can't sell that!'

Master tapes were carried out the door.

T.C.

I got a radio show on 3mFM in Inverloch and played demos and outtakes of records I had worked on, explaining how they were made. People would ring up the station indignant!

'Who do you think you are, talking about these people as if you know them?'

Old friends would come to the farm to visit, like Billy Miller. We did a few recordings on a Teac 4-track in the tin shed out the back. For some reason cows like feedback and drums. When we were working they would saunter down the hill and stand alongside the fence, chewing. It must be pretty boring being a cow! Once Upon a Time came to record. They were a band from West Berlin, friends of Mick Harvey. Their singer, Bruno, was Bronwyn Adams' brother. He had an operatic voice which was bizarre but very good. Bruno was stoked with the results, and the cows were too.

Tony and Billy Miller in Kongwak, 1989.
Image by Claudia Carey, courtesy of Billy Miller.

I also recorded Wild Pumpkins at Midnight in that shed. It rained all day long, absolutely poured. You can hear it throughout the record. The rain on the roof is as loud as the music.

T.C.

I was in Kongwak when the Berlin Wall came down in November 1989. Blue Ruin had contacted me to work on the album *I'm Gonna Smile*. Phill Calvert, their drummer, was the connection.

Blue Ruin's singer, Quincy, had some funny stories. He was working in a retirement home as a nurse at the time and there was an old bloke with balls that hung down to his knees. Quincy was taking him to the toilet and accidentally jammed the lid on his balls, so the old boy belted him with his walking stick.

'Mind the testicles!' he roared.

Quincy did in future, he was most careful.

The sessions for *I'm Gonna Smile* were unremarkable, but I did like the band's anti-drug songs. They sunk into my memory, I suppose because I could relate to them. We mixed the album in Studio 3 at Metropolis in January 1990. Armstrong's had changed its name again and was now run by Ernie Rose. Armstrong's, AAV, Metropolis – it gets a bit confusing. It was forever Armstrong's to me.

Ernie had finally completed Studio 3 in 1988. There was an overdub booth to the left and a big control room with SSL desk, luscious speakers and beautifully sound-crafted rock walls. It had fantastic acoustics. The desk was mounted on a turntable so you could rotate it 180 degrees to mix for film. On the back wall were three speakers, left-centre-right, which became the front, and the two main speakers became the rear. It was a big kerfuffle to turn the desk around because of the cables, but it was brilliant and well ahead of its time. I did some of my best mixing in that room.

Blue Ruin were a good band – I don't know what ruined them. I saw them play live a few times and thought they were better onstage than on record. It wasn't that the band recorded badly, but they were more exciting and dynamic live. They played some great shows, I think I even mixed some.

T.C.

The girls I'd meet were interested in music and recording, like my wife, Astrid Munday. She knows how it works. Astrid is a singer and songwriter who contributed backing vocals for artists including Grant McLennan. That's how we met, they were friends.

Tony and Astrid Munday, 1991. Image courtesy of the Cohen family.

Watershed was recorded in Sydney in September 1990. The sessions were straightforward. I had demoed much of the material the year before with Grant and Robert Forster for The Go-Betweens' proposed follow-up album to *16 Lovers Lane*, before the band split. Grant knew what he wanted and didn't need much input from me. Just get a good sound, that's how I remember it.

LISTEN
'When Word Gets Around'—Grant McLennan

I would often use silly names for songs and albums, some artists would laugh and others not. I called *Watershed* Watercloset, just to annoy Grant. For some it was insulting their art, but others just thought I was a funny bastard.

T.C.

Things got more serious as my health straightened up.

In February 1991 I returned to Sydney to record Bhagavad Guitars and decided to stay. The band was on a label called Red Eye, run by John

Foy. I would soon produce a number of bands for Red Eye: The Cruel Sea; Beasts of Bourbon; Kim Salmon and the Surrealists; Tex, Don and Charlie. It was time to get back to work and make some good albums, and maybe even a bit of money!

I'm fascinated by how The Cruel Sea started.

As far as I know, Tex Perkins was their lighting engineer. They were playing gigs on harbour cruises as an instrumental band and Tex saw them and dug it, so he started turning up to shows and doing their lights for fun. Of course, things grew until he began singing every now and then, putting lyrics to their music and that's pretty much how it stayed. Tex is a very charismatic frontman and he found a good vehicle with those guys. They were brilliant musicians, and their songwriter Danny Rumour was an absolute gem. He once told me that adding lyrics to his music was like putting a red nose on the *Mona Lisa*, which I thought was an incredibly funny insult.

The Cruel Sea would always include instrumentals, but a whole album of that would never have got much success. It was Tex's vocals that brought the band recognition.

T.C.

In April I moved to Bondi with Astrid. The Cruel Sea had recorded an album on 8-track called *Down Below*. It's fantastic. More and more songs were getting lyrics and it was decided that I would produce their next album.

I had an absolute ball.

This Is Not the Way Home was recorded at Megaphon in Sydney, a studio overlooking the airport. The plan was for it to be a natural recording, with nothing too fancy. The studio had empty factory space so I decided to use it as reverb chambers. You can hear it on the album – the combination of different reverb sounds and time lengths creates depth and dynamics, helping to paint a picture. It was great that the studio allowed me to do it, or that I got away with it.

LISTEN
'This Is Not the Way Home'—The Cruel Sea

I'd put reverb on drums, vocals, backing vocals, sometimes percussion, but it would depend on the song and instrumentation. For example, kick drums with reverb are great, but not on fast hits. The reverb turns into swill. But if it's a slow hit? *BOOM!* The reverb dissipates and then *BOOM!* Just like John Bonham recording 'When the Levee Breaks' in a stairwell. I love those stories, innovation is half the fun. Most times I managed to get my experiments right. I must have, otherwise the band would have said, 'Oh no, that's not what we want.' Which happens, too, of course.

This Is Not the Way Home was recorded quickly, with minimal drama, and became quite successful. I knew from the very beginning I was onto something special with The Cruel Sea.

T.C.

Beasts of Bourbon's *The Low Road* was recorded in Studio 2 at Metropolis. It came together easily and the album was mostly live. It's a good recording and not particularly because of anything I did, but because the band was in a happy place.

A great deal of what's worthwhile happens in the moment. Bands seem to hit a peak and if you manage to get a recording during that time there's not much you can do to spoil it. I hadn't worked with Beasts of Bourbon in eight years. With new members Brian Hooper and Tony Pola, the band were working well together as a group. Sure, there were moments of volatility, but there always was with Tex. He could be a prima donna! As long as the vocal sound was good he'd be happy. Vocals nice and loud.

Tex is a brilliant singer, one of the best to record.

I've tried a number of microphones on vocals, but there are only a few that I like. Neumanns are good, the U87s and U89s, but it depends on what sound you're looking for. I love M49s, they are rich – provided the valves are changed regularly. Otherwise they can go dull. Tex would sing with the mic halfway down his throat, so I'd use a Neumann TLM170 on him. He'd blow all the others up. Tex has a fantastic quality of voice, rich and deep, but he can also make it tear if he wants. I don't think he's ever been taught, it's just instinct. He knows how to work a microphone.

T.C.

Mixing is not a formula or something you can preconceive and I don't think it ever will be. It's the result of an interaction between a certain group of people and the music.

The lyrics affect it of course.

By the time it came to mixing I knew them well, and if I didn't understand what they were about, I'd ask. Some of the answers would surprise me, but 'Chase the Dragon' is obvious. 'A souvenir all the way from Kampuchea' was Spencer Jones' lyric. Tex was always concerned that the country no longer existed, but he couldn't come up with anything else that rhymed.

LISTEN
'Chase the Dragon'—Beasts of Bourbon

Spencer's guitar is in the left speaker playing the riff and Kim Salmon is in the right, with Brian panned in the middle. Their groove is spot-on. The mix then came together as the recording did, I just turned everything up and got the EQs right.

And found those reverbs.

Some drummers have excessively loud hi-hats that ruin snare drum sounds, so you gate the snare drum microphone to remove them, then put a bit of reverb on to cover it up. It was never an effect I was fond of, but you did it to get a decent sound. A couple of reverbs become the core of your mix and things fall together around that.

T.C.

Einstürzende Neubauten toured Australia in July with Beasts of Bourbon as support. Roger Grierson was their tour manager. The first place they wanted to go when they arrived was the tip, to get rubbish to bang and smash. And they did. There was a broken shopping trolley onstage that they hit with iron bars. I remember Roger saying he thought he'd heard it all until someone started yelling, 'More shopping trolley! Turn up the shopping trolley!' That was a new one.

Sin Factory

(1991)

Once you develop a taste, it's hard to stop.

I went on tour with The Cruel Sea in September. Tex has very funny footage of it, but some parts are best not shown. There's scenes of us taking drugs and him shoving the camera in everyone's face. Touring can be fun in exotic cities, but driving around the back roads of Australia the novelty wears off. We spent hours in the minibus annoyed we were there – well I was anyway. There's footage of the late roadie, Speedy. He's driving us through a deserted country town in New South Wales when a kid comes down the main street riding three skateboards, stacked on top of each other. Someone calls out, 'Turn around, Speedy, let's knock him off!' We didn't, of course, but were so impressed we went back for another look.

It was the highlight of the tour.

T.C.

The only time The Bad Seeds used a 'real' producer was for *Henry's Dream*. They were advised by their record company to try things differently, so got David Briggs. He was a big-time American dude who had produced Neil Young's records. It was a wash-out.

I'd left Sydney and moved back to Kongwak for a rest. I was on the farm when the phone rang.

'Hello, Tony, it's Nick here. Do you remember me?'

We hadn't seen each other for a long time.

Tony in Kongwak, 1991. Image courtesy of the Cohen family.

'Oh yeah,' I replied. 'I remember you. Aren't you that old punk rock singer?'

Nick explained that the band had recorded *Henry's Dream* in Los Angeles at the end of the year and were now back in Australia. He'd been listening to the mixes and didn't like them.

'They don't sound very good,' he complained, 'and we were wondering if you could come in and fix them up?'

That phone call launched me back into full-on work.

On *Henry's Dream* The Bad Seeds learnt to get the performances right. Prior to that they'd record the songs, and the mix – the final process – would make everything sparkle. Briggs pushed them to play better, take after take after take. The performance was everything. Apparently he would stand in the middle of the studio, surrounded by the band, playing air guitar while they recorded. Can you imagine?

I would never have done that. Pushing the band certainly made for better records, but I wouldn't have felt comfortable telling Blixa Bargeld he's not doing his job. Like, what is his job? He makes crazy sounds.

T.C.

We started mixing at Metropolis in January 1992. It had been almost four years since I'd worked with the band, so there was plenty of doubt, in particular from their record company, Mute. I'd developed a bad reputation.

You don't pay someone to not get results.

I never felt any artist was a client, but you're hired to do what they want. With Briggs the band had paid a lot of money for a bit of show. He had got them to perform well, but when it came to the mix, Briggs left all the faders at a certain spot and that was it. For him, the performance was the mix. That did not work for Nick Cave, it sounded dull. Things need a boost. That's what I learnt from Molly – exaggeration.

We spent a couple of weeks in the studio comparing mixes and making changes. I've always been a fan of hard panning. If there's two guitarists, I like to mix them on either side to create a stereo image. Quite often you have to, or the sound becomes unclear. Mick Harvey wasn't such a fan of that and I'd often catch him moving the pan control toward the centre to make it less full-on. He usually won.

I'm not sure where we panned Briggs' air guitar!

We were back in business. It was obvious to everyone that we should get back together as a team, particularly Mick. The heroin barrier wasn't there and we were having fun. Nick got merry one night and wanted to call Briggs. We had to tie him down or it would have got nasty.

T.C.

I don't like talkback buttons, I've never been a fan of communicating that way. 'Blah, blah, blah. Do this, do that.' I'd rather walk into the studio and have a conversation. I'll look at the guitarist's pedals, look at the microphones. See what's going on in there. Besides, I ran into several problems with talkback buttons that didn't switch off.

An incident with Greg 'Tex' Perkins is one that I remember.

The Cruel Sea's 'Black Stick' was recorded at Perth's Planet Studios in March. The band was on tour, so they flew me over. We were sitting in the control room waiting for a microphone to be fixed, discussing different names when 'Greg' came up as a rather silly-sounding name. The talkback button was on, so Tex heard all this out in the studio.

'Whoops, sorry, Greg!' I said.

'Black Stick' is a great vocal. Tex performed the whole song in one take on acid, just as the trip was coming on.

LISTEN
'Black Stick'—The Cruel Sea

We finished the session at about 5 a.m. and went back to the hotel. It was so bloody hot. Tex came in a bit later and went out on the balcony and started squawking at the crows.

'Oh fucking shut up will you!' I shouted.

'Sorry,' he replied. It was most unlike Tex to apologise, the acid must have made him peaceful.

T.C.

I believe in the psychology of a recording session and like to meet the band beforehand to get to know them. The pre-production meeting for TISM's *The Beasts of Suburban* album was a strange experience. I arrived at a big house on Punt Road in Richmond and was greeted by about fifty people. TISM were anonymous, adopting stage names and wearing balaclavas, so I had no idea who the band members were.

I turned to the person next to me and asked, 'What do you do in the band?'

'I dance a bit,' they replied.

I turned to another. 'And what about you?'

'Oh, I'm the drummer.'

'And you?'

'I've got nothing to do with these people at all!'

It was only as we recorded that I found out who was in the band.

TISM made me laugh. They were really well organised, perhaps too well organised compared with other musicians I'd met. For a start they all had jobs – they were lawyers, doctors and dentists. Singer Peter, aka Ron Hitler-Barassi, was well and truly out of control. At shows he would jump up on lighting rigs that hung precariously above the crowd. It was a sight to behold, from a distance.

T.C.

We recorded *The Beasts of Suburban* at Atlantis Sound in April. I'd already worked at the studio on albums for Charlie Marshall and Stephen Cummings. It was great and took over where Richmond Recorders left off.

At Atlantis musicians would drop in all the time, but TISM were very professional. They came to the studio in shifts. During mixing there would be two band members in the control room at all times. I'd have my head down in the desk, turn around and see them sitting behind me. I'd turn around a few hours later and there were a different two sitting there! They recorded me slagging them off. I don't recall how that came about, but they thought it was hysterical and put it on the end of the album:

Absolutely hopeless, I hate them. TISM lacks the sheer guts of anything like say The Beasts of Bourbon. I mean there's a gutsy band. Of course their cheap sarcasm, it pretty well doesn't get there. It's not real good. It doesn't approach the epic sort of comedy and wit of The Birthday Party.

Mourningtown Ride (TISM)

I did enjoy TISM. We worked together again on the *Australia the Lucky Cunt* EP, but someone else remixed it. The band said that I made them sound too nasty. I thought that was amusing.

T.C.

Kim Salmon wrote half the Beasts of Bourbon songs and knew how he wanted them to be, so there could be conflict. In Kim's other band, Kim Salmon and the Surrealists, he was the frontman.

The Surrealists' album *Sin Factory* was recorded in July at RBX Studios in Richmond, which was where *Young Talent Time* had ended up after Richmond Recorders. It was a quick recording. The band at that stage was Kim, with Brian Hooper and Tony Pola – the rhythm section of Beasts of Bourbon. Tony was a volatile character. One night he threw a full beer can at Kim's head, narrowly missing, and stormed out of the studio!

Motivation is a big part of recording.

Say 'Yes, you can do it' or 'Maybe try it this way?' And if ego is involved, the best thing to do is to convince people it was their idea. Reverse psychology, it's not that difficult. Most singers I worked with recorded a live vocal as a guide for the band. I could be wrong, and sorry if I am, Kim, but I never felt he was confident with his vocals. He came back and recorded many of them again. I think Kim has a really good voice, it's distinctive and that's exactly what you want from a singer.

We started mixing at RBX, but the sound of the control room wasn't ideal. Some studios are like that and mixing becomes guesswork. You think to yourself, *What's this going to sound like outside the studio?* That uncertainty was easier to deal with when I was working in Melbourne because I had a stereo at home I would use as a reference.

T.C.

Some record companies and even artists themselves aren't aware of the differences from one studio to another. Control room monitoring is important and it's rare to find an accurate room. I finished mixing *Sin Factory* at Atlantis. The studio wasn't flash, but it delivered good results. I could trust what I was hearing.

Kim and I got along well. He was good to work for and left mixing decisions to me. I had free rein, which was a great deal of fun. It's good to indulge oneself occasionally.

LISTEN
'Rose Coloured Windscreen' — Kim Salmon and the Surrealists

Sin Factory is a fantastic record. I would go at it all night, keeping myself awake with drugs while Kim fell asleep on the couch at the back of the control room. I'd drive him home at sunrise and he would arrive later in the day and say, 'Yeah I like that, it sounds great!' And so it went, me taking speed and drinking a bottle of Jack Daniel's every night. That's not a great way to treat your pancreas and liver, especially for someone with hepatitis C.

I never said I was smart when it comes to my health.

After completing *Sin Factory*, I went to the clinic for my methadone. Astrid and I were renting a house in Windsor, opposite the bowling club. As we walked up Chapel Street I started feeling sick, but we bumped into Dave Graney so I stopped for a chat.

'Come on,' Astrid said. 'You haven't got time to talk now!'

We made it to the clinic and I collapsed. I was hauled off to hospital, where doctors discovered I had pancreatitis. I was only in for a few days and left as fit as a fiddle. Unfortunately, the pancreatitis led to diabetes – but it would be a couple more years before I found out about that.

T.C.

Atlantis was a strange place. It was located underneath the King Street Bridge in South Melbourne, exactly where Crown Casino is now. It had a very heavy industrial vibe.

The studio became the black hole of music in Melbourne.

Charlie Owen was often there. At the time he was playing with Maurice Frawley and Shane Walsh in Working Class Ringos. I'd worked with Maurice back in the 1980s at Richmond Recorders with the band Japanese Comix. He cropped up many times. Maurice was a country boy, very laid-back and brought with him that attitude to recording. 'This is what I do, don't change it.' I understood that straight away and never tried to impose on him. All Maurice wanted me to do was capture his music.

Whoop Whoop was recorded at Metropolis in September and mixed at Atlantis the following day. Charlie always got involved with the mixing and we had good control. Maurice wasn't precious with how his songs were mixed and never stood over me saying, 'Oh no, too much reverb on this, that or the other.' His main concern was with how the band played the songs, something they'd iron out well before recording.

The Honeymoon Is Over

(1992)

Atlantis was run by Dave McCluney. He was a generous, sensitive bloke who could relate to artistic people and he let them record cheaply. It wasn't a great business decision, but it was great for musicians. Everyone felt welcome.

I had some very enjoyable sessions at Atlantis and worked with wonderful people. Bart Willoughby's band Mixed Relations came through in October. It was a great experience and my introduction to Aboriginal musicians. The album *Love* was recorded at Glebe Studios in Sydney. I flew up on 3 October. It was the day of the Victorian state election, so I voted at the airport.

'Best of luck, Joan!' It didn't do her much good, she lost.

The recording was quick and painless. The band was natural and laid-back, which makes for great results. They had soul.

LISTEN
'Take It or Leave It'—Mixed Relations

Bart is a funny character and told me a great story about touring Europe. He was stuck at a railway station somewhere in Germany in the freezing cold and all he had with him was his handmade drum kit, so he burnt it to keep warm. I think that's beautiful – why worry about earthly possessions?

Mixed Relations didn't do as well as I expected, I thought the band would go much further. Bart invited me to go fishing with him in Broome and I'm going to take him up on that one of these days.

T.C.

You can make average music that you don't believe in sound okay, but it's hard work. When the artist is good you don't have to do much at all. The sound is already there. There's nothing you can do to spoil the record, you can only make it better.

That is a joy.

Tex, Don and Charlie's *Sad but True* was recorded at Metropolis in November. It was very quick. Tex Perkins, Don Walker and Charlie Owen are fine musicians and don't need twenty takes to get it right. Warren Ellis and Jim White appeared as guests on the album and had just started playing together as Dirty Three. I came across Warren many a time. He played violin and flute on Kim Salmon and the Surrealists' *Sin Factory*. Warren does strange things with a violin and has an uncanny knack of knowing what will work on a recording. He can listen to a song once, then go out and play. That's not at all easy. He's passionate and has a touch of madness that makes him really good.

Recording a classy drummer like Jim you can get a good sound without putting gaffer tape anywhere near the kit. Occasionally I'd put a microphone down near his drum stool. He liked to hear his old bits and pieces creak and squeak because it was part of his sound.

T.C.

For many years I was convinced I couldn't go into a studio and work without speed. It was a psychological addiction, whereas heroin was a physical addiction, and it took me a very long time to overcome.

Robert Forster's *Calling from a Country Phone* was recorded by Dave McCluney at Sunshine Studios in Brisbane. I was booked to mix the album and busy working at Metropolis when the phone rang – it was the owner of Sunshine Studios. He sounded like a nice bloke, but unfortunately caught me in a very bad mood and I behaved like a rude, arrogant bastard.

'I've got a good little studio,' he started. 'It's got a low ceiling and is very acoustically—'

'I bloody hate low ceilings,' I interrupted. 'I like big rooms!'

He called me back a week later.

'I just wanted to let you know the workmen have come in this morning and are raising the roof.'

I didn't know what to say. He was raising the studio roof a couple of feet, which wouldn't make much difference at all. I felt so bad.

When I arrived at the studio to mix the album I couldn't make sense of the mixing desk. It took me two days to work out and after that the session is a blur. I had been waiting on a package from Melbourne to improve my alertness and was checking at the front desk every ten minutes. 'Is the mail in yet?' I'm sure the hotel receptionist guessed what I was waiting on, how could they not? When the package arrived all hell broke loose.

The mix went well. Robert sat outside in the lounge area reading a book most of the time. He'd come in and listen, do a little dance, then go back out again. It was odd at first, but I came to realise if Robert was dancing he must be happy with how things were going.

T.C.

I worked with Dave Graney on *Night of the Wolverine* in December. We clicked well. Dave didn't have a big budget, so we completed most of the backing tracks live in a day at Metropolis. That's probably what makes the album good. It sounds stress-free and rolls off the tongue.

LISTEN

'Night of the Wolverine 1'
—Dave Graney 'n' the Coral Snakes

We moved to Atlantis for mixing. By then I'd started working on The Cruel Sea's *The Honeymoon Is Over* and The Bad Seeds' *Live Seeds* concurrently. It was a great time, the height of Atlantis. Many people were coming and going and Dave, like anyone else, would grab whoever came through the door and put them on the record. Tex Perkins performs a monologue on 'Night of the Wolverine (reprise)' simply because he dropped by the studio.

'Would you mind singing on this?' Dave asked.

'Yeah, no worries,' replied Tex and got straight to work.

Dave was really happy with *Night of the Wolverine* and I think it's one of his better records. He said it dragged him from the gutter up to the penthouse where he belonged. Funny bugger! His next album, *You Wanna Be There but You Don't Wanna Travel,* was more difficult, we didn't establish the same flow.

T.C.

Live Seeds was a collection of live recordings from The Bad Seeds' recent European and Australian tours. We started working on the album in January 1993, just Nick and I in the main studio at Atlantis.

You wouldn't guess the vocals are rerecorded.

Nick wasn't happy with what he'd performed live. Back then he would leap about the stage and carry on like a goog, so he sounded out of breath. I played the backing tracks through the monitors in the control room and turned it up loud to emulate a gig. With a Shure SM58 stage microphone Nick sang the vocals live, or I should say re-sang them. I don't know how we managed to record without his microphone feeding back, the speakers were belting like crazy! I sat huddled at the desk wearing a pair of big old-fashioned headphones – unplugged – just as ear protection.

LISTEN
'From Her to Eternity (Live)'
—Nick Cave and the Bad Seeds

I let the tape roll and Nick sang from start to finish, then I would change the reels and record the next fifteen minutes. To his credit he didn't stop, he performed one complete take. It was as though he was onstage. Mentally, he was. His eyes were shut and he ran back and forth behind me in the control room screaming and doing his thing, without having to worry about entertaining the crowd. He sang exactly like he would live.

Except not as out of breath, or badly out of tune!

It was good fun. The recording worked because it was a live performance, rather than really faking it and doing a studio vocal. A big cheat wouldn't have worked. This was just a little cheat.

T.C.

As was the case with Richmond Recorders, Atlantis became a good place to score. Let me state, though, that had nothing to do with Dave McCluney. He was a straight, clean-living chap.

At Atlantis it was always music first.

Hangers-on don't bother me. They are usually friends of the musicians recording and their only desire is to watch people they respect doing what they love. I find no harm in that. Besides, I'm good at switching off. If there's a racket going on I don't hear it, I focus on what I have to and block out the rest – it becomes part of the job.

Atlantis had two control rooms, with the recording room in the middle. As I mixed *Live Seeds* in the main control room, the band was in the recording room writing and learning material for what would become their next album, *Let Love In*. Dave was recording it all in the small, shittier control room down the hall. I remember looking into the recording room to see at least twenty people carrying on. There was Dave Graney, Tex and the guys from The Cruel Sea, and all these other people sitting around playing bongos, tambourines and god knows what else. They were having a great time.

Some of the demos from that session came out so well we later used them as rhythm tracks. One certainly did, 'O'Malley's Bar', which appeared on the *Murder Ballads* album. Strange how some recordings come about.

T.C.

Sessions for The Cruel Sea's *The Honeymoon Is Over* had started at Metropolis back in November with Danny Rumour and James Cruickshank. Danny had a vision for the album. I have great respect for artists like him who can see a finished product. Some of the sounds on the album are him playing a six-string acoustic guitar as a bass by putting it through a graphic equaliser.

At the time, I was tired of good musicians not getting a chance. Record companies would pour money into big bands, but an unknown alternative act like The Cruel Sea was dismissed as 'indie' music, which radio and television wouldn't touch. There was very little on the radio outside of the mainstream. Everything was safe. Luckily there were independent stations like 3RRR in Melbourne, or the government station triple j in Sydney, which began to expand nationally at the end of 1989. That changed things. Suddenly people were exposed to music they'd never heard before.

And they liked it!

By the time the Big Day Out festival went national in January 1993 things had changed a great deal. *The Honeymoon Is Over* marks the point where Australian record companies started taking more risks, and that meant employing people like me.

T.C.

To this day I am in awe of Fairchild compressors, they have an amazing sound. I hired some for the recording of *This Is Not the Way Home* and *The Honeymoon Is Over* and couldn't stop raving about them. Next thing, they were popular and I couldn't get hold of one.

Me and my big mouth!

Mixing is really big stuff and I only started to get a grasp on it in later years. *The Honeymoon Is Over* had a good budget, so I had access to gizmos I hadn't in the past, which was fun. I preferred to be left alone, but I do like the artists around to finish things off. In fact, I came to insist on it. There are a million directions a mix can take and it helps to have somebody else there to decide. After all, I don't write the songs. Danny was always in the control room hovering over my shoulder, putting his two bob's worth in. He was very pedantic.

The sound of The Cruel Sea was somewhere between Beasts of Bourbon and a slick pop group. That was difficult because Tex wanted it tough, while Danny wanted sweet guitar sounds. As the producer it's your job to strike a balance so everybody in the band feels like they're getting their ideas across without too much compromise. You approach it as a negotiation until there is something, hopefully, resolved. I found I was reasonably good at that. I'm diplomatic, or at least I used to be.

Tex was never interested in technical stuff and didn't want it explained. One night he'd had enough and threw a control room chair at me. That sort of behaviour wasn't unusual – I was grumpy, we all were. The Cruel Sea were on their way up and the pressure was on. This album had to be good.

T.C.

I can be accused of spending too long on a mix, but I do know when to stop. It's just that sometimes my vision is a little further than others can see. *The Honeymoon Is Over* was mixed for radio appeal. That was my doing and I took it very seriously. I wanted to prove that The Cruel Sea could be commercial.

I made the album sound so good that radio had to play it!

The band made fun of me for being obsessive, which I probably was. The mixes took a long time. I'd spend three days on one song, just to perfect it. At Metropolis one weekend I went so hard I passed out. The assistant engineer came in and found me face down on the mixing desk. He picked me up, blood dribbling down my face and put me on the couch at the back of the room. I slept for a few hours, got up and headed straight back to the mixing desk. He came in saying, 'No, no, no', and marched me out to the foyer, called a taxi and sent me home.

The band returned to the studio on Monday and thought I'd gone mad. I was sitting at the desk with a round scab in the middle of my fore-head, fiddling with the snare drum sound. They shook their heads, appalled. It looked as though I'd spent the entire weekend working on one sound. I hadn't, I'd been fiddling with everything until I was satisfied.

LISTEN
'The Honeymoon Is Over'—The Cruel Sea

I was really pleased with *The Honeymoon Is Over*. It was a deliberate attempt to get airplay, and it worked. The album became a hit. Engineers and producers still tell me they love the sound of that record, which is good. I never did find the bit of my brain I left on the mixing desk.

T.C.

Atlantis was a hangout, as I imagine the old Black American studios were. Like Chess Records' Ter Mar in Chicago and Motown in Detroit, there was often something interesting happening. Unfortunately, Crown Casino leased the surrounding Southbank site in the middle of 1993 and that was the end of the studio. It was a shame. Dave's business partner, Jim, thought he might be able to squeeze some money out of the casino as compensa-tion, but he was dreaming. That's not what casinos are about – hitting the jackpot is only for them.

They're greedy bastards.

Let Love In

(1993)

It's true I am a little mad, but years in a recording studio will send you around the bend. Still, it's a healthy kind of madness. I don't go around chopping people up with chainsaws.

It's more a feeling of vagueness.

I've spent so much time in the control room. Days. Weeks. Months. Years. It's a padded cell. When working on an album I become fanatical and channel my attention completely. That's my way, I don't know any different, but it comes at a cost. I lose touch with reality and the world outside becomes a dream. People ringing up wanting to sound like Nick Cave, offering their dole cheque in return. Negotiate the next deal, pay the rent, there just wasn't time. I was too busy in the studio. Eating, that's another thing I'd forget. So I got myself a manager, which took a world of pressure off.

T.C.

Tiddas' *Sing about Life* was recorded in Studio 1 at Metropolis in April. It's a beautiful album and I often wonder how I came to be working on it. I guess the band heard something I'd recorded and liked the sound, or maybe someone recommended me. I certainly didn't know much about them.

Sing about Life was an unusual record for me. It was out of character, a completely different style compared with other albums I was working on at the time. It was a great education and the experience probably calmed me down. There were no Molly Meldrums carrying on, Nicks punching you in the face or Texs throwing chairs. It was a fun, easy session.

LISTEN
'Tokoua' — Tiddas

Band members Sally, Amy and Lou were the sweetest people. We recorded part of the album live in front of an audience, which was moving. They had a lot of friends, there must have been more than fifty people there. I had an assistant engineer at the time, John Brewster, who was a well-known roadie. He did a fantastic job running the PA, but had a terrible speed habit. He looked scary, running about the studio chewing his gums incessantly, so I had to pull him aside.

'John, just take a breath and calm down,' I implored.

We kept it fairly simple, mic'd up their voices and guitars and off they went. They performed a concert, which was recorded to 2-inch tape.

Tiddas had a terrific didgeridoo player, Froggie. He went with John to record some didgeridoo tracks with natural reverb, so they set up under a bridge in Richmond. Of course, the police turned up to find out what was going on. I realised later that was a close call because Froggie had a problem with authority figures. I don't know what had happened to him in earlier times, but he obviously hadn't had a good run of it. One day he consumed too much and collapsed outside the studio. An ambulance arrived, but when Froggie saw uniforms he flipped out, thinking they were cops. When the police did come, in this instance, they were just trying to help.

T.C.

The doctor called.

'I have to talk to you,' he started, 'but we can't do it over the phone. You've got to come in.'

No one wants to hear those words. I freaked out and went on a huge binge, assuming I had AIDS. When I finally saw him he told me I had diabetes.

Listen to your doctor. If I had taken my diagnosis more seriously I'd be in better shape than I am now, but I was in denial. Like most people, I thought, *No way, this is not going to fuck me up.* What a dickhead. I remember at the time feeling immense relief that I didn't have a terminal illness. Unfortunately, it took me some time to realise that diabetes was a chronic disease I'd have to deal with for the rest of my life.

T.C.

Michael Turner was a friend for a long time. I mixed Wild Pumpkins at Midnight's *Going Sick* at Metropolis in May. You can hear Tiddas singing on the album.

I like to get acoustic guitars sounding fat and bright. Whatever studio you're in, go for the best microphone they have. Put it as close as you can without getting in the guitarist's way, just around where they're strumming, and use compression if necessary. That depends on the player. I sometimes capture a room sound to put the instrument in another space within the mix, but it has to sound natural. If you've got the luxury of an acoustic guitar with a good pickup, record that to another track. A pickup captures frequencies which, when you blend them together with the microphone, give you a powerful sound.

LISTEN
'Beautiful Sick'—Wild Pumpkins at Midnight

I capture not just an acoustic guitar's bass frequencies, but loads of treble. I then put more treble on, as much as I can lay my grubby hands on! Treble is so important. Rub your thumb and index finger together close to your eardrum. Hear that trebly sound? That's what brings recordings to life. I'd put instruments through a BBE Sonic Maximizer and get extra sparkle I didn't know was missing.

T.C.

If you're ever in London and you like reggae, I recommend the Notting Hill Carnival as a great thing to observe. It's chaos! There are people everywhere and stacks of speakers playing completely different music. If you don't stand directly in front of a stall you get very disorientated.

Astrid and I were staying in Notting Hill ahead of recording Nick Cave and the Bad Seeds' *Let Love In*. It was a bad time – an ambulance had to come and take me to hospital. The ground was shaking with bottom end as the paramedics drove through the carnival crowd. When I arrived at hospital I was put on insulin. I didn't look grey anymore, so I knew I had to start taking it. The amount I have to inject has gone up over the years. My pancreas doesn't produce any natural insulin now.

The sessions for *Let Love In* started at Townhouse 3, South London, in September. The studio had previously been named Ramport and owned by The Who, who recorded *Quadrophenia* there. Townhouse 3 had a Neve 8078 console. I love Neves for recording, they have a wonderfully warm EQ. The session lasted a few weeks. After the experience of *Henry's Dream*, Mick Harvey had become very focused on capturing good performances of the songs, which made him more of a taskmaster.

The piano on 'Do You Love Me?' sounds like drawing pins in the hammers, but it's not. It's a Steinway grand – if I had put drawing pins in that I would have been lynched! By then I was using a Neumann SM69, a lovely stereo microphone with two U67 capsules, to record pianos. I would put it a couple of feet above the piano, back from the hammers and angled nicely. Then I added two Crown Pressure Zone Microphones, which are very trebly, right above the hammers with one at the top and one at the bottom, gaffer taped onto stands. I EQ'd any remaining bottom end out of the PZMs to make the sound bright and used it to highlight the attack of the hammers, blending in the SM69 for richness. There were all sorts of phase problems to deal with, but it was worth it.

That piano sound did me well on many recordings.

T.C.

I throw up ideas all the time, as is required. If you're too frightened to speak you're not someone Nick would want to work with. Most of my ideas are rejected, but occasionally a good one pops through.

A noise gate is a device which switches audio off below a set threshold. As an effect, it doesn't do much for me, but I love to trigger gates from an external input. You can hear the sound at the start of 'Do You Love Me?' That's Blixa's guitar triggered off Thomas' snare marching beat. Blixa had a rack of gate devices, running one into another, and set the threshold so whenever there was a loud snare hit, his guitar leapt out.

He told me it was the best guitar sound he'd ever had.

Thomas played the drums brilliantly. On his snare I'd use an AKG C414 microphone switched to supercardioid to keep the spill out. They've got a 20dB inbuilt pad, so can also handle loud and noisy snares. I'd use a Neumann U47 FET on the bass drum if it could cope with the level and, if not, an Electro-Voice RE20 or something similar. I position it just inside the shell. I've never liked bass drum microphones such as the AKG D12, they're not bright enough. Bass drums have treble in their sound too! I like Neumanns on toms. For hi-hats a Neumann KM84 or whatever they're called. I often forget the model numbers. The overheads were Neumann KM100s. They are a mini KM84 with an interchangeable capsule and clip to put them on the perfect angle. I position them right above the kit and close mic the ride with whatever is left lying around, a KM84 or something. If you're recording in a good room you can go berserk with room mics, like a pair of Neumann U89s or the SM69.

We finished tracking the album and did a short tour of Europe. It was fun – the wives and girlfriends came along. Nick was successful by then, so we travelled in actual buses and I didn't have to drive!

T.C.

On 19 November, Ernie Rose was at the Sydney Cricket Ground record-ing *Madonna: The Girlie Show – Live Down Under*, the first Australian performance of her world tour. I was at Metropolis working on Maurice Frawley and Working Class Ringos' album *Livin' Lazy*.

I often wondered how people like Madonna managed to sing while dancing and leaping about the stage like a maniac. Lip-syncing, that's how they do it. Ernie was alarmed to find that Madonna had eighty tracks of vocals prerecorded for the show. When she'd get puffed out, the front-of-house mixer would turn up the required vocal. It was a harbin-ger of the slow death of live music. By contrast, I'd watch Maurice play in the front bar at the Esplanade Hotel in St Kilda on a Saturday after-noon for the price of a pot of beer.

When he was on form he was mesmerising.

Maurice was extremely modest – he was a great songwriter, an absolute genius. Unfortunately, though, my memories of us together are fuzzy. Maurice was a tortured artist and fought hard with his demons. He would spend time in the country and stay in good health, then come to the city for gigs and get fucked up. To his credit he was good onstage, he'd stand and deliver before he got bent. He wouldn't fall over out of it, though maybe after the show we would! There's not a bad word to say about Maurice.

T.C.

When Nick's in frantic mode he sets up camp, usually around the piano and his artwork spreads from there. You can see it on the inner sleeve of *Let Love In*. Nick tore up bits of paper and gaffer taped them to the wall, then as the pieces got too big he moved out into the corridor and god knows where else.

Let Love In was mixed at Metropolis in December.

I can't visualise much of those sessions because we got up to no good. Nick was coping with more work at one time than I had seen. He was enjoying the challenge, and when Nick's enjoying himself, everyone else does too. He was an inspiration and spurred me on. We worked like we used to, cramming in a twenty-hour day with four hours to recuperate. It was wild. After a few hours' sleep I'd crawl out into the sunrise, my eyes would shrivel up and I'd head back into the studio again. I felt fully confident and the pressure of a deadline added to making the record good.

T.C.

When I listen to Nick Cave records I think the credits should read: *Mixed by Tony Cohen and Mick Harvey.* It was a partnership. I knew how to make gizmos work, but Mick knew when there was too much or too little.

He had a very clear idea how the band should sound.

Mick never wanted to spend too much time on mixing. As far as he and Nick were concerned, you get a song to a stage where it sounds good and that's it. I guess they're right, but on *Let Love In* I took my time. Nick always liked to listen to mixes loud on big monitors. By then I'd found a compromise: the Yamaha NS-40s. They were good – twice the size of NS-10s and the sound was more colourful. They were certainly fucking loud! Don't forget to check your mixes at low levels to see where the cymbals and other high-frequency sounds are sitting because you hear differently at loud volumes.

I used a lot of reverb on *Let Love In* and improvised with effects to create sounds I could hear that weren't present in the recording. It's interesting and comes across well, but I wouldn't do it like that these days. I'd go a lot drier. But it worked at the time.

LISTEN
'Do You Love Me? (Part 2)'
—Nick Cave and the Bad Seeds

I remember Nick playing back the album when we had finished, as is his custom. It's a purge. He stands in the middle of the control room, listening at a level not many human beings can stand. I'd made my way to the other side of the building and I could still hear it! I was proud. We'd made a beautiful record.

T.C.

People tell me an album is great and I think, *Yeah, it's got some great tracks on it, but a great album?* That's rare. I don't enjoy listening to my work, I'm too critical. I hear mistakes, or what I consider mistakes, and things I could have done differently. There's always something you will find. I don't lose sleep over it, though, because I know nobody else would notice or even care.

You're too close to the work and have to let it go.

I listen to an album again six months later. By that time usually it has been released, so what I don't like about the recording can't be changed. I can then hear things differently and enjoy it for what it is. Sometimes I realise the album is quite good! I'm not just talking about what I did, but the effort of everyone involved. It might have been lost on me at the time as I was too busy concentrating on capturing the performance and doing what I thought would sound right.

I've worked on hundreds of records. I am often happy with individual songs, but there's only a small percentage of albums I enjoy as a whole. I listen back to those and think, *Wow! That's really good.* When that happens, the feeling is as good as it gets.

T.C.

'This is an award I think I richly deserve.'

That's what I said when I won my first ARIA. I guess it sounds arrogant, but in truth I'm piss-weak at talking about myself. It isn't something that comes naturally. I get nervous and need a push.

I won Producer of the Year in March 1994. It was the culmination of a great run: *Sad but True, Night of the Wolverine, Live Seeds, The Honeymoon Is Over, Sing about Life, Going Sick,* and I'd just finished Powderfinger's debut album, *Parables for Wooden Ears.* For me, though, the award wasn't just about those records, it was an acknowledgement of twenty years of work. I even mentioned Molly in my speech, given he insisted he'd got me into the business.

'I beg to differ,' I joked. 'I had a bloody good job in a studio before I met you!'

Molly was amused. He thought it was great I had the cheek to contradict him – all in good fun, of course.

It was an important time for music in Australia, things were changing. Tiddas won Best Indigenous Release and so much happened for The Cruel Sea. The band crept into the mainstream and sold a lot of records. They won ARIAs for Album of the Year, Song of the Year, Best Group and Single of the Year. After the ceremony they said, 'Sorry, Tony, we realise now what you were trying to do. Thanks, it did us good.' Their apologies were graciously accepted. It felt good to be recognised and gave me a boost.

I'd managed a big budget and come up with a good result.

The after-party was interesting, full of people from the industry getting drunk and making fools of themselves. It was a jerks' turnout, as Ian Davis would have said. Tex jammed one of his ARIAs into the wall. He was carrying on like a popstar and good on him. Unfortunately, he left without the award and someone pinched it.

Murder Ballads

(1994)

Mainstream record companies didn't want anything to do with me because of my association with punks and underground bands. 'We can't use him. He's a scallywag, no good.' When I won my ARIA it felt like I showed them. Just because I wasn't working on pop records that were going to make a lot of money, or music a certain label based in Melbourne would be proud to put out, didn't mean it wasn't good.

Most of the artists I worked with made music I liked. After the ARIAs, bigger acts started approaching me, but I wasn't excited by them. I didn't want to go that way. Sure, there might be money and prestige, but they weren't making records I considered great. Let them stick with their regulars, the producers from overseas who come to Australia and charge through the nose. I finished up work on a Daddy Cool reunion album with Ross Wilson, Ross Hannaford, Wayne Duncan and Gary Young and went to Townsville with Astrid to visit my brother, Martin.

T.C.

Kim Salmon and the Surrealists' self-titled album was recorded at Metropolis in the middle of 1994. Beasts of Bourbon had played their final show in December the year before and Kim quit the band.

I always loved working with him.

The things that guy can do with a guitar! I put him in the same boat as Rowland and Blixa. A bloody genius. Most guitarists worth their salt have got their sound and it's not up to me to work it out. Kim had his. He'd put down his amp, plug in a wah-wah pedal and there it was, a great guitar sound. All I had to do was get a microphone and record it. Sometimes, though, the sound was a product of the mixing. Kim would record his guitar and I'd run with it, following the sound he led me toward. That was so much fun.

LISTEN
'Redemption for Sale'
—Kim Salmon and the Surrealists

You've got to have valves for some things. All the best guitarists have a valve amp in their collection – Kim did. I don't think he ever thought why, he just knew that it sounded better. I'd mic his amp with a Neumann U47 FET, if it was available. If the sound was really loud and a condenser microphone couldn't suffer it, I'd use a Shure SM57. In a good-sounding room there might also be an ambience microphone further away. If not I'd simulate a room with digital effects. They're more controllable, and sometimes better. When mixing, one channel would form the main sound, with others blended in for colour, depending on the song. Each sound would add another dimension.

T.C.

I recorded a cover of the Tom Waits song 'You Can't Unring a Bell' with These Immortal Souls at Metropolis in October. By now my health was starting to fall apart. Diabetes was taking a toll and I would get burnt out more quickly. It's a shame but bad luck, I did it to myself.

In later years a co-engineer handled the technical stuff.

I joined The Cruel Sea for *Three Legged Dog* at Megaphon in November. The band had toured Europe supporting The Bad Seeds and were now writing as a group, with Tex at the helm and Danny moving to the back. Paul McKercher co-engineered *Three Legged Dog*. It gave me time to sit back and listen. When you're operating the desk you have to concentrate on machinery, as well as listening and communicating with the artist. Now I could just focus on production.

LISTEN
'Better Get a Lawyer' — The Cruel Sea

'Better Get a Lawyer' is a fantastic single. It's a rip-off of the Jon Wayne song 'Texas Jailcell', you can see it mentioned in the credits. We got the best bass sound. Megaphon had a concrete stairwell. The bass amp was set up in the studio but had an extension connection, so we ran a lead down the stairwell to a second speaker. The sound was magic! I couldn't use it for the whole song or the bass would become a blur, but every now and then I blended it in with the amp in the studio. The stairwell acoustics added bite, and the sound ripped.

The Cruel Sea went back on tour and *Three Legged Dog* made it to number one. I thought that if the band could remain friends they had a chance to be absolutely huge. I hoped so. They would be not just rich, but well loved.

T.C.

Eventually Nick Cave had his own researchers. A team of people he trusted, well-read types like Mick Geyer. They got along famously. Mick would stay on Nick's houseboat in Chelsea, London, and work with him all the time.

I introduced them to each other. When I came back from London in 1989, Mick got in touch with me to write a book about Nick. I was drying out, so he came to the farm. I liked him. He was a smart bugger, with a quick wit that left me in the dust. I'd be dribbling syllables while he waxed lyrical! Eventually he and Nick became friends, which was pleasing. But there's no free lunch, everyone has to pull their weight. If you're around Nick and he respects your intelligence, he'll set you to work.

Nick thrived on Mick's input and it gave him some time back. Nick would provide Mick with references to books and while Nick was busy doing what he does, Mick would look them up. It makes sense, much like someone researching a book. An assistant writer, if you will. I wouldn't be surprised if some lyrics are Mick's, though I was never privy to their conversations.

T.C.

Mick Harvey started his Serge Gainsbourg cover albums *Intoxicated Man* and *Pink Elephants* a few years prior and would record whenever he could get a studio and an engineer. I remember doing some of it overseas, but mostly in Melbourne.

Mick played many of the instruments himself.

Tracking becomes automatic because you know what's going to work and what isn't. *That's the sort of microphone I'd like on this, and that's the sort of microphone I'd like on that.* It comes naturally, rather than something you have to labour over. When you're working with someone who is building up a song incrementally it is more difficult. You can't hear how the song is supposed to sound when all the instruments have been added, so it's a matter of imagining, or knowing, what is going to work.

The best thing to do is capture as much sound as you can from the instrument you're recording, and if it's too much, pull it out later. When it comes to mixing it's always best to subtract frequencies. Sounds are difficult to put back in – think back to James Freud's snare drum. You don't want to be finding a concrete corridor to re-amp a snare drum every mix!

Victor Van Vugt completed the Gainsbourg albums. We didn't talk about things, just did our separate work. I found him a bit competitive. By then I'd decided to stop engineering. I'd just be a producer and mixer. I figured that's the time you really get to have some fun.

T.C.

The Café-Bar was a crap low-tech plastic instant-coffee machine made in Australia. Metropolis had one installed and when every studio was booked, an odd assortment of characters would meet at this place in space and time.

I'd often have a peek to see who was lurking about.

Nick Cave and John Farnham together making cups of coffee? That's oil and water. There were some very funny combinations. I remember Nick and Joe Calamari, sorry Camilleri, standing at the Café-Bar wearing exactly the same cardigan. It was a black-and-red zigzag affair, so they must have shopped at the same Kmart. I gather Nick wasn't impressed because he changed out of it fairly quickly. I have mentioned this a few times, but Nick has a great sense of humour. A lot of his music is very funny and *Murder Ballads* is one of his best. The lyrics are hysterical. It's tongue-in-cheek, black humour that makes me laugh to this day.

Nick Cave and the Bad Seeds mixing *Murder Ballads* at Metropolis, 1994.
Left to right: Blixa Bargeld, Mick Harvey, Nick Cave, Tony, Conway Savage, Martyn
Casey and Thomas Wydler. Image by Pierre Baroni, courtesy of the artist's estate.

Murder Ballads was recorded at Metropolis by Victor and me. Nick had a completely different vibe for the album – it was a free for all, which worked brilliantly. The only thing I didn't enjoy was recording the backing vocals.

I always found them difficult. The people I worked with would be in the studio performing together, laughing and mucking around. On 'The Curse Of Millhaven' it was Nick Cave, Martyn Casey, Conway Savage, Thomas Wydler, Warren Ellis, Brian Hooper, Spencer Jones, Dave Graney, Katharine Blake, Clare Moore, Rowland Howard, James Johnston, Ian Johnston, Geraldine Johnston and Astrid. I had to go through the tape and manually erase all their talking and laughing! It was entertaining, but hard work.

I named them The Moron Tabernacle Choir.

T.C.

During a dinner break at the studio one evening, Nick came in and proudly presented me with a gold record for *Let Love In*. The band thought it was a great hoot, but I was chuffed. I'd never received one before. Mum's got it put away somewhere, I think I was using it as a breadboard.

I started mixing *Murder Ballads* in December and completed much of it on my own, which was unusual. I'm not sure where Nick's head was at, but he didn't seem to worry. In fact, I was still mixing the album when he returned to London. I had relocated to Gotham Audio, a studio near Ringwood which belonged to John Farnham. It was peculiar – the control room had a large window that looked out at gum trees. The view was lovely, but very different to the dark caves to which I was accustomed. I'd watch the trees as I mixed and call Nick up in the middle of the night.

Quite a few tracks were left off the album.

The snare on 'Stagger Lee' sounds like it was run through a SansAmp pedal. Distortion is a great trick. You can make sounds appear to be thundering even when they're soft. I first used the pedal in 1993, after Mick Harvey had purchased one for the *Let Love In* sessions. Mine came from a pawn shop and was beaten up. I started using it as an effect on snare drums, cymbals, vocals, all sorts of things. Anything except guitars, which is what the pedal was actually designed for! It created great sounds, strange things you didn't expect and seemed to have a mind of its own.

I still have my SansAmp pedal, but Mick moved on to the Line 6 Pod. He loved it because he could have all his sounds saved as presets. I think he ended up not using an amp onstage at all, just the Pod and some foldback.

T.C.

The duets on *Murder Ballads* were overdubs. Kylie Minogue appeared with Nick on 'Where the Wild Roses Grow', which surprisingly became a hit. It did them both good – Kylie gained credibility and Nick gained commercial exposure. The song has proved to have longevity.

I occasionally see the video on television late at night.

Kylie had a squeaky-clean image and it was Nick's black humour to record a song about him murdering her, with Kylie singing along. As far as I know she jumped at the idea. Blixa Bargeld recorded a guide vocal of Kylie's part and her only request in the studio was a jar of lollies. Good on her, I reckon that's cool.

LISTEN
'Where the Wild Roses Grow'
—Nick Cave and the Bad Seeds, Kylie Minogue

I finished mixing *Murder Ballads* in early 1995, but wasn't happy with 'Where the Wild Roses Grow'. Kylie's voice was too sibilant. I rang Nick in London and told him, so they got someone to change the mix. I could have kept my mouth shut, but I'm glad I didn't. What's best for the record is best for everybody.

I've lost a lot of sleep over sibilance. It drives me up the bloody wall. Most singers are fine, but some have sibilant voices and it's very difficult to remove later. De-essers are designed for that purpose, but create a lisping sound. Nick would have found himself dueting with Ita Buttrose! If someone has a sibilant voice it's best to fix a pencil, vertically, to the front of the microphone when you're recording to protect the capsule.

I saw Nick and Kylie perform 'Where the Wild Roses Grow' onstage at the Big Day Out in Melbourne the following year. Nick was quite graphic with his gestures. I wound up in a Fred Negro cartoon about it. 'Are you going to the Big Day Out to watch Nick grope Kylie's tits?'

T.C.

Ampex made great tape machines, you could really slam the meters. Half-inch 2-track was the best to mix to because the wider the tape, the more sound you can pound into it. I get teary just thinking about it. Funny what moves one sometimes! I never liked noise reduction and found it adversely affected the sound. Tape hiss? Who cares.

I would prefer to have always had a say in who mastered my work, but it depends on many factors: the record company, budget, politics. Of course, there was Don Bartley in Sydney. I would use him whenever I had the chance – he understood what sounds I liked to get. We worked together often, which helped. As I got to know Don we would discuss the mastering over the phone. That was much better because flying to Sydney for an afternoon wasn't my idea of a good time. Instead, I would send him the mix on half-inch analogue tape, with a DAT backup and notes.

'So you want the usual?' Don would ask.

'Oh yes, thanks very much.'

Mick Harvey would attend mastering sessions and was very keen. Nick wasn't. He didn't need to be there to sing or play, so didn't care. 'Do whatever you want, just make it sound good.' Really, Nick? Oh no, we wouldn't do that!

Murder Ballads was mastered in England, as were many of Nick's later albums. They did a good job. Don had started working less. He wasn't young – back then anybody over forty was considered old, says me now.

T.C.

Fortissimo was a studio in South Melbourne, near the corner of Dorcas Street and Kings Way, which was owned by Andy Parsons. It didn't have flash equipment, but I always got good sounds out of the place.

The Blackeyed Susans' *Mouth to Mouth* was recorded by Victor at Fortissimo and mixed by me. I remember coming in late every day, then disappearing to the toilet for half an hour. 'Feeling a bit crook in the guts,' I'd say, thinking I had everyone fooled.

LISTEN
'Let's Live'—The Blackeyed Susans

I always start mixes with the drums, soloing each track and applying EQ until the sound fits close to everything else. Kick drum, snare drum, then overheads. I try to isolate the toms, but can hear from the spill what frequencies are required. Once the drums are done I bring in the bass and get the rhythm section going. The kick drum and bass should sit in a similar place, depending on the song. I then bring in the guitars and everything else to get an overall picture. The rhythm section may sound fantastic on its own, but along with the other instruments it sounds like shit. If so, you've gone the wrong way, so start again. Once I have all the sounds set, I then think about compression.

An instrument might jump out where it shouldn't.

I respected The Blackeyed Susans, they were great musicians and prepared to experiment. I played wah-wah on 'I Can't Find Your Pulse', which the band thought was funny. An instrument sounded good through the pedal, so I stuck it under the desk and played the effect during the mix. I love showing off!

Gone

(1995)

Metropolis was my favourite studio, so it was awful to see it go. The history of Australian music seeped from the walls. Many would never have had a career if it hadn't been for Bill Armstrong, Roger Savage and Ernie Rose.

For me, it was also the place I had grown up.

Large studios like Metropolis were a product of their time. They had a lot of equipment and staff, which meant a lot of overheads. By the middle of 1995 the studio was in trouble. As Alesis Digital Audio Tape (ADAT) became popular, competition increased, recording budgets dropped and large studios everywhere started struggling. Bit by bit Ernie was forced to close the facility down. Studio 1 was the first to go, the big room that fitted a symphony orchestra. The control room was kept in use as a mastering room, but the recording space remained empty. It's a shame, but I suppose things change. Albert Studios on Pitt Street in Sydney is another important piece of history that's gone. It's a car park now.

Albert's closed in 1986 and moved to North Sydney. Its new location was a sterile, corporate place. Almost a jingle studio. How depressing. I rerecorded 'Turn Up Your Radio' at Albert's with The Masters Apprentices and Hoodoo Gurus in April. I knew the original recording well. It had been engineered by John Sayers at Armstrong's back in 1970. It's just as well I didn't think too much about that at the time, or I would have been intimidated. The original 'Turn Up Your Radio' was recorded on 1-inch

8-track. Now – twenty-five years later – we had state-of-the art equipment, so the recording quality would, of course, be superior.

I very much disagree with that sentiment now. Two-inch 16-track recordings sound better. Ampex, Studer, I've still got a soft spot for those machines. Optro not so much, though if you had a 16-track Optro now you'd have something of extreme value. As a novelty item.

T.C.

I won ARIAs in two consecutive years.

Astrid and I arrived at the Convention Centre in Sydney in October for the ceremony. The technical awards were handed out before the televised event, and as we were walking down to find our seats some guy read out '… and the something or other of the year goes to, Tony Cohen!' At the time, I was having a hypoglycemic episode – a 'hypo' – which is caused by a low blood sugar level. When you have a hypo you shake and perspire. I was dripping wet, so the last thing I needed was to stand onstage in that state trying to explain myself. No one would have believed me. Instead, I turned around and walked out of the venue.

I'd won Producer of the Year and Engineer of the Year.

It's a shame I couldn't accept those ARIAs. I know Molly was disappointed. He was standing on his seat in the front row, casting his eyes about yelling, 'Tony, where are you? Where are you?' I was at the back of the Convention Centre half-unconscious. Hypoglycemia makes your brain stop working because sugar is what fuels it. I've stood in 7-Elevens desperate, staring at the lolly counter not knowing what to buy. It's ridiculous – you just eat the first thing you see and you're fine.

There were a few things I wanted to say that night. I never thought I'd win an ARIA but after receiving a few I no longer saw it as honourable. It didn't feel right. The technical awards may be honest, but the rest? Look at some of the artists who win. For them it's a marketing and promotion exercise, a music industry wank. I was told record company representatives would meet and say, 'Well you had last year, we want this year', then decide which one of their acts were going to win. I hope that's changed, in the meantime I use my three ARIA awards to hang my washing up to dry from the curtain pelmet in my caravan. They're very heavy.

T.C.

Saying 'yes' can sometimes be a big mistake.

I was in London recording *Hustle into Bed* for the British band Delicatessen. They were lovely guys, but nothing to rave about, and we were booked in a studio I wasn't happy with. The control room monitoring was difficult and there was bugger all I could do about it because the session was paid for. At the same time, Dirty Three were in London recording and very keen to get me involved. I liked the band, they were making innovative and interesting music, so I was excited at the opportunity to work with them. *Fuck it*, I thought. *I'll just take a few days off from Delicatessen.*

How stupid. I should have told Warren Ellis, 'Sorry, I can't do it. I've got a gig.' Instead, I was greedy and tried to work with both bands at once. No matter how hard I tried I couldn't be in two places, so neither band knew where I was and the whole thing turned to shit.

I left Dirty Three sitting in the studio without an engineer.

It's unfortunate, but Delicatessen had paid for my flights, so my responsibility was to them and I had to go back. I wasn't happy with how *Hustle into Bed* came out. I hadn't done my best work, which was a shame.

T.C.

In 1995 Charlie Owen joined Beasts of Bourbon on guitar. I'd been working with him in Sydney on Tex's solo album *Far Be It from Me*. I didn't see Charlie as a Beast of Bourbon. I don't know why, I guess it just wasn't what I was accustomed to at the time.

We recorded *Gone* at Seed Studio in South Melbourne.

I've always loved the sound of different rooms – stairwells, cupboards, toilets. Whenever someone records a vocal in the toilet they are compelled to flush at the end of the take. I have no idea why. Once or twice it may have remained on the recording. There were two toilets at Seed Studios, so we set up Brian Hooper's bass amp in one to isolate the sound. I always record an amp along with a DI signal straight off the pickup. Adding a little of the pure sound adds depth and helps give the instrument presence.

When using a DI you often have to press the phase reverse button, which always freaked me out. Why were the two signals out of phase? I never did understand. Was it the time it took for the sound to get to the DI as opposed to the nanosecond longer it took to go through pedals, into an amp and out the speaker? Or was it the EQ? Maybe the leads were wired the wrong way around. I recall agonising for hours over whether I preferred the sound in phase or out of phase, in phase or out of phase, in phase or out of phase. I'd just keep pressing the phase reverse button until I figured out which sound I liked best.

I usually EQ the bass and compress it on the way to tape, with settings to make it pump. If it's an average bass player I'll have the sound a little lower in the mix, but I've been lucky. Most of the people I worked with were good, like Brian Hooper – he was the hippest of the hepcats! Brian played very loud. When we were packing up at the end of the session, I opened the toilet door and the plaster roof above his amp had collapsed.

T.C.

'Saturated' was written by Charlie and Ian Rilen. Ian was a lovely guy, and I don't say that only because he's no longer with us. He would always greet you with a warm smile and his arms outstretched wide. It was an honour to have known him.

LISTEN
'Saturated' – Beasts of Bourbon

Spencer Jones plays lead guitar on 'Saturated'. It's a great song, but I'm sorry to say the album was ill-fated. I stole something from Tex, so he sacked me. It doesn't matter now, we seem to get along alright. It was a bad time for me, I was speeding so much. Sometimes that was the only way I could get the job done.

Tex sacked me over the phone, which was dumb. He left a message on my answering machine. 'Tony, it's Tex here. You're fucking sacked!' That was it. What could I do but sample it? It was a gift. I made a loop and played it to anyone who was interested, not to Tex's pleasure I'm sure. He certainly had a temper. To his credit he's calmed down a bit these days and is a rather nice bloke. He probably wouldn't like me saying that! Some compare Tex to Nick Cave, but I don't see the similarity at all. Of course they're both fantastic singers and a joy to have in the studio because of their brilliant recording technique, but that's where the similarities end. They are each unique.

T.C.

I received royalties for *Murder Ballads* and took time off. Astrid and I married in 1997. We recorded three albums on no budget whatsoever and I think they're pretty damn good.

Her first, *Astrid Munday*, was recorded at Atlantis.

Dave McCluney had set up a new studio in Hawthorn. While he did engineer at the old Atlantis, he tended to leave it to others. Dave began to engineer more and more as a result of necessity. Mick Harvey became friends with him and saw his potential, so kept working with him as he honed his craft. He saved Dave's skin not only by bringing work in, but by paying him properly, which is one of Mick's really good traits.

Astrid's album was recorded quickly. Some great musicians appeared on the album as favours here and there. I played synthesiser on one of the songs, 'Speed of Light'. She was silly enough to let me! It's good, a one-take fluke I performed on my Roland SH-101. They're great instruments to drive people mad. You can set the sequencer, turn it up and go out for the day. What a prick of a neighbour I must be. I don't do things like that anymore, nor think I ever did, but I often thought about it. I gave that synthesiser to Charlie Owen years ago.

T.C.

ADAT first appeared in 1992. It enabled you to record eight tracks of digital audio to one S-VHS tape. I recorded Astrid's album at Atlantis to three ADAT machines linked together.

They were awful and went out of sync all the time.

When digital recording first appeared I was keen, but I never took to it. I found it prissy. Misusing equipment was part of the creativity of recording. With analogue you could thrash the meters and natural tape compression would make the sound better. I miss that. Dare to slam a digital meter into the red and see what you get? It doesn't distort, it glitches. Digital took away things that I enjoyed, but it did make recording cheaper and easier for artists. I set Astrid up in the front room of our house in Windsor with ADAT machines and she recorded the rest of the album herself. It was good, she could fiddle about as much as she liked and if something went wrong call me in.

LISTEN
'Playground'—Astrid Munday

I wish Astrid had better luck. She appeared on the television show *Recovery*, just her with a guitar, but she was nervous so it didn't come across as well as it could have. Performing on live television is difficult if you're not accustomed to it.

T.C.

Recovery was a hip, new live music program on the ABC on Saturday mornings. At that time there was almost no live music on television in Australia. *Countdown* was long gone and the variety show *Hey Hey It's Saturday* was for major label acts.

It was an amazing time for alternative music.

Recovery was one of the most peculiar things to happen at the ABC's Ripponlea studio since *Countdown*. It had a similar format, with young schoolkids coming to see their favourite bands up close and personal. Chris Thompson was the show's live producer and would get me in when he wasn't available. I'm glad he did because it was good fun! Jon Spencer Blues Explosion played on the show in September and smashed up the set. It caused a real stink and the cameramen threatened to walk out. I was in the recording truck outside watching on a small black-and-white monitor, howling with laughter. It was a great performance.

{WATCH}
'2 Kindsa Love (Live on Recovery)'
—Jon Spencer Blues Explosion

Recovery went to air at 9 a.m. and ran for three hours. I had no idea what was going on at that time of the day, nor did most of the bands. Frenzal Rhomb ran amok. They stayed up all night after a gig and got really drunk. The band was starting to sober up as showtime drew near, so they sent a roadie off to get more booze. The only place you could get alcohol at that time of day was the Railway Hotel in Windsor, a twenty-four-hour bottle shop. The roadie returned with the goods and the band were shit-faced by the time they appeared. They attacked the host, Dylan Lewis, with a razor and tried to shave his head. It was considered bad form, but very funny.

T.C.

I didn't have a car, so would be at Windsor station at 7 a.m. to catch the train two stops to Elsternwick, a five-minute walk from ABC's studio. One morning I arrived affected by amphetamines, talkative and in a particularly good mood. The producer started chatting with me to organise a regular spot on air. 'You'd be perfect,' he enthused.

I ran away from that.

'No, mate, it's artificial,' I countered. 'You should see me when I come down.'

Me, a television presenter? Yeah right, that'll be the day. The new Molly Meldrum! That's what some said of Dylan.

He was terrified before he went on air, which surprised me a great deal. You wouldn't know it to watch him, he looked so natural on camera, but he was outside the studio chain-smoking. On one occasion we were evacuated. It was twenty minutes before the show was due to finish and someone rang up claiming they'd planted a bomb, so staff ushered the audience out and cleared the studio floor. Everyone was huddled on the street away from the building while the police came in with sniffer dogs. People watching at home must have been amused when a documentary about emus suddenly appeared! They likely thought it was part of the show, but Dylan never reappeared to finish the episode.

I got to know some of the *Recovery* crew well. Tim Millikan was the front of house engineer, the foldback guy. Now he's one of the best live engineers in the country and does concerts with monstrous PAs. Tim has a shack in Tasmania on the same lake as Chris Thompson. One day we'll end up as old, deaf engineers trout fishing.

T.C.

When recording I loved the Yamaha REV7, SPX90 and SPX900 for reverb. Even the AMS RMX-16 was great for some things. I'd still use them today, but when mixing there's nothing better than the Lexicon 480L. I'd reach for it every time and was never disappointed.

If you ever see a music documentary with some dude waffling in a studio, there, at the top of the mixing desk, will be the remote of a 480L. They first appeared back in 1986. I always preferred effects that didn't require you to fiddle with the parameters. The factory settings should sound great and the 480L had four or five I loved – great vocal and drum reverbs. I'd flick through to find a setting that worked, then make it sound better by adjusting the parameters. There were far more than you needed.

The 480L was easy to use and even some of the novelty effects sounded good, which is really saying something. Usually they bug you. I particularly loved the stereo tremolo. If you got it in time with the music, you could create a good left to right, drive-people-nuts sound. It's fun to run one effects unit into another. I would often plug a SPX90 with a phasing effect in line with a reverb, just to provide movement. You don't hear the actual phasing sound in the mix.

T.C.

I've always worked on instinct. It's not a boast, I just never had a clear idea what I was doing. I would follow what the artist led me toward, and if not I'd make something up. Perhaps from memory.

LISTEN
'Always Round Here'—Lodger

Lodger was Pearl Lowe and Danny Goffey, with Neil Carlill and Will Foster from Delicatessen. They flew me to London to mix their debut album *Walk in the Park*. Danny was the drummer of a much bigger band, Supergrass, and Lodger was his pet project due to his influence with the record company. He was a funny little bloke and had a decent two-up two-down in London, so obviously had some money. Danny liked his drugs too.

No More Shall We Part

(1998)

In February I began working on Cold Chisel's reunion album *The Last Wave of Summer*. It had been fourteen years since the band split and Don Walker was keen for me to get involved but Jimmy Barnes wasn't, as usual.

The band's reunion was a big secret.

I arrived at a rehearsal room at the Opera House in Sydney and a sign on the door read *Australian Taxation Department*, a band in-joke. Jimmy had returned from living in France after some trouble with the taxman. They rehearsed for quite a while and Jimmy seemed to be in charge, but not much was getting done. Finally we moved to Festival Studios and started recording. I'd never had such a big budget. I could have anything I wanted, and Jimmy always wanted more. There was a mixing desk to monitor the headphones and another to feed the multitrack.

LISTEN
'This Time Round'—Cold Chisel

Jimmy was always on the go and didn't hang around. He ran in ready to work and when he was done he ran out again. Watching him in the vocal booth was the best part. He made me laugh, pulling faces. I'd be getting a vocal level and he'd break into a reggae version of the song! He disappeared for a week when his wife sent him to India to see a guru and get off coke.

T.C.

Roger Grierson had just been put in charge of Festival Records. He'd worked his way up and become a music industry bigwig, with a fancy office and an inflatable clown he used as a punching bag.

Don and I were in the studio downstairs and went off for lunch. Roger wasn't in his office but the door was open, so we went in and sat the clown in his chair. I thought he would laugh, but he got quite cross. Once he found out Don was involved, though, he shut his mouth. I have a lot of time for Don Walker. He always made an effort, even for scumbags like me. He was fascinating to talk to, so articulate and wise. You wouldn't believe he played in a rock band! I loved our coffees together in Sydney. Every afternoon he would chat, drink coffee and puff on a big expensive cigar.

I love to see a person enjoying their poison.

Don and his wife were a very hospitable couple and always happy to have me over for dinner. They lived at the bottom of Kings Cross in the posh part, Elizabeth Bay, next door to former prime minister Paul Keating. Don's house was on a smallish block so there were lots of stairs and, at the very bottom, on a flagstone floor, sat his grand piano.

T.C.

When we started mixing the album at Metropolis, Jimmy took the mixes out to his car to compare them against The Rolling Stones' *Exile on Main St*. To me that made no sense because he was comparing apples to oranges.

The Last Wave of Summer is a recording of a band playing live and, unlike The Rolling Stones, there were no brass instruments. If I had mixed the vocals as low as Mick Jagger's on *Exile on Main St* Jimmy would have had a heart attack! He certainly liked himself to be heard. I never felt confident enough for Cold Chisel. Don and the other guys I could dig, but Jimmy was hard. He wasn't happy unless the mix was running through ten different machines. I had top of the range compressors and equalisers stacked high in the control room and he would come in and say, 'They're for the vocals are they?'

'Oh yeah,' I'd reply.

Some weren't even plugged in. I'd become so used to working with little, I couldn't figure out what to use them on. Eventually I got sacked and the band took the album to New York and mixed it with Kevin Shirley.

Jimmy always liked big-name American dudes.

It hurts when an artist decides to go to someone higher up the food chain. Thankfully, I heard back that Kevin couldn't find much wrong with my mixes. 'What should I improve on?' he asked. 'What can I do that's better?' That made me feel better and, most importantly, I remained friends with Don.

T.C.

I was never charged for studio time at Fortissimo. Instead, Andy Parsons and I would do favours for each other. Astrid recorded her second album, *Apparition*, there. It was good, I had cleaned up a bit. I certainly wasn't pure, but I'd improved my health and even managed to give up smoking.

I would sometimes play percussion on Astrid's recordings. If there was ever a chance to rattle and shake something I'd be straight into it! I love what it can add to a song. Think back to early Beatles records with the tambourine loud in the mix, *CHICK-CHICK-CHICK-CHICK*. It's beautifully played and really powerful. I was never that great, but I did have a good knack. I played the hand drum on 'All You Need Is Sleep' from Tex Perkins' *Dark Horses* album. I spent all night on it, so was most upset when Charlie Owen forgot to credit me. The truth is, I was never meant to be on the other side of the glass. As the pressure mounts I start to freeze. I can only perform when no one is watching.

LISTEN
'All You Need Is Sleep'—Tex Perkins

I liked Andy and Fortissimo was great, while it lasted. Unfortunately, though, I slipped back down the slope, reacquiring vices and took Andy with me. Things got pretty fucked up. Andy was a bass player in the Victoria Police Band, believe it or not. He wasn't a policeman, but had a badge as an honorary cop. That was quite amusing considering our fondness for certain substances.

Andy was a good engineer and together we recorded *Since You've Been Gone*, a solo album for Cold Chisel's Steve Prestwich. Or we tried to. Steve was a very talented man. He had ideas in his head of how he wanted the album to sound, but he didn't get the right people involved and tried to play many of the instruments himself. The sessions became increasingly disjointed and the album fell apart. I'm sure I was no help – Steve had struck me at a fairly bad time.

It's okay to peak, but don't over-peak.

Andy went too far and ended up in debt. He had to get rid of the studio and his mother sold her home in England to help pay the bills. She came over and dragged him back to clean up his act. It's a sad story, but has a happy ending because Andy returned to Australia and is doing alright.

T.C.

For a long time I had a good manager in Russell White. He was a lovely man but left the music industry, largely because he wasn't mean and cold-blooded enough. Even so, he did what he could for me.

An engineer gets paid a flat fee, while producers get royalties. I didn't understand what that meant in the early days. I got paid well at the time, but I used it in an inappropriate way. It was foolish, but money wasn't something I was interested in.

I wish it had been.

The issue I now have is that I can't work and therefore have no income. That's the problem with not working, it doesn't pay very well! I recommend you get a cast-iron contract when you record because it's not the bands you're dealing with, it's their managers and record companies. As the producer I was supposed to get royalties for The Cruel Sea, but somehow it didn't happen. I received $1000 once – big deal. The only band that has consistently paid me producer royalties is Nick Cave and the Bad Seeds. Mick Harvey always kept an eye on things. He was interested in the music business and it's just as well because they could have been ripped off as much as every other band.

So it's due to Mick I receive royalties. There was never an agreement with the band's label, Mute Records, but he made sure I got included. I can't thank him enough.

T.C.

After I won the ARIAs I considered moving to America. I wanted to try out big New York studios and boss their engineers around. I would beat the Yanks at their own game! Instead, Astrid and I moved to London in 2000.

Hansa Tonstudio in West Berlin was bettered only by Abbey Road. It was the greatest studio I ever worked in. The Bad Seeds had recorded their previous album *The Boatman's Call* there with Flood, so I first visited the studio for mastering. It was heaven. By that time everything was digital, but Abbey Road had kept their record lathes, which would prove to be wise. That equipment was being trashed everywhere, people didn't want it anymore, but as it turns out things come back into fashion. Even vinyl!

Sessions for *No More Shall We Part* began in September.

Abbey Road had everything that opens and shuts. You walked into the microphone cupboard and it was the size of a house. There was every mic ever invented, in pristine condition and fifty of each. I was blown away. We were recording in Studio 2, which was The Beatles' studio. Talk about a kid in a candy shop. I sat on the recording room floor at three o'clock in the morning in awe. It was too much – John Lennon had sat right in that spot all those years before, fiddling with a riff.

Abbey Road is a bizarre place. The front fence gets covered in graffiti, with people from all over the world coming to leave messages. Every month it gets painted white then covered with writing again. One morning I was standing at the entrance having a smoke. I had long hair, an overcoat and round sunglasses. Japanese tourists started taking photos of me through the mist! Yes, I know what they were thinking.

T.C.

I've spent so much time running in and out of control rooms making adjustments that I should be really fit. Abbey Road was particularly exhausting because the control room is at the top of a staircase.

I was knackered with all the running back and forth!

Spill is the sound of one instrument leaking into the microphone of another. It's always a problem and the cause of lost sleep. Just one of the many things about recording that makes you go mad, eventually. Abbey Road was difficult because Studio 2 is one big room. To isolate instruments they had huge screens made of white acoustic tiling with a glass panel in the middle. They were probably around in The Beatles' times, which freaks me out.

We put Nick's piano in the centre of the room, with screens to separate the drums. Nick's vocal would spill into the piano and vice versa, which was a problem if either got rerecorded, so we put covers over the piano. It didn't matter in the end as we kept both the original piano and vocal. In later years Nick's best performances were always when he was playing the piano and singing at the same time. It did limit my options, I couldn't EQ his vocal how I might like, but who cares. A better performance makes for a better record.

LISTEN
'Love Letter'—Nick Cave and the Bad Seeds

Headphone mixes can be difficult, especially when you have multiple sends and you have to keep switching between each to see what people are hearing. By now musicians could create their own headphone mix, which was a double-edged sword. It was good for engineers as it gave us one less thing to worry about, but some musicians you had to overrule.

Thomas Wylder could never work it out. He has trouble with his ears, which is not uncommon for drummers. The high frequencies from cymbals do some damage. I remember Mick sat at the drums, put on headphones, hit the snare and almost went deaf! Thomas had turned everything up so loud that he was only tapping the drums. That makes it difficult to get a good drum sound, so I went and fixed his mix, but when I came back an hour later he'd fucked it up again, no two ways about it.

T.C.

There are people who prefer the sound of analogue and insist on using it. I'm one of them, but I do understand it's not something everybody can afford, particularly when there's an alternative. I like to think it will become popular again.

I usually record at a tape speed of 30 inches per second, but it depends on the budget. Two-inch tapes are expensive, so many albums were recorded at 15 inches per second, which has an EQ bump in the bottom end. The budget for *No More Shall We Part* was good, so we recorded everything to 48-track at 30ips, which was two 24-track tape machines synced together. That was a luxury and meant I could put room microphones on things I normally wouldn't. Whether they got used in the mix I can't remember.

At Abbey Road you got as much help as you could want. During the sessions I played back a tape and what I heard differed from the input. The sound wasn't as deep. It was not a huge difference, but a difference none the less.

'Where's the bottom end on the bass drum?' I said. 'It doesn't seem right.'

Next thing, an army of technicians in white lab coats invaded the control room and threw us out.

'Bugger off,' they said. 'Go and have a rest.'

We sat and had a coffee while technicians checked the tape machines, only to find it was a dodgy batch of tape.

'Well done, you heard it!' they complimented, shaking my hand.

I was proud, but I think they were just relieved there was nothing wrong with their equipment.

T.C.

No More Shall We Part was mixed at Westside Studios. I wish we had stayed at Abbey Road, but it was expensive and had gobbled up a large part of the budget. Westside was a tin shed by comparison.

It's good manners for a studio to ensure there is an assistant engineer to help out. Sometimes, particularly in England, there wouldn't be, and unfortunately Westside was one of those studios. I struggled with the mixing desk. Westside had a modern Neve VR console, which I didn't know much about. It was fully automated, which meant the faders moved. That was frustrating. Every time I touched something it would be remembered, so faders were moving up and down all the time. Mick Harvey turned to me and exclaimed, 'Wake up, Australia! What are you doing?' It's the only time I can remember feeling out of my depth in a studio.

I was having health troubles, too, which didn't help and I would keep disappearing to the hospital for diabetes checks. I became overwhelmed and started thinking I better not take on projects so big.

T.C.

I have the vocals in early when mixing, but working on the actual sound is one of the last things I perfect. Depending on who it is, that can be a long or short process. Vocals are so important. I lose interest in a song if I hear someone mumbling away in the background. With some exceptions, the vocals should be the loudest thing in the mix.

Clear and up front.

Nick liked a present vocal, but effected with a delay or short reverb. I got a vocal sound for him on one track which was really in your face. I thought it sounded great, but he took it home, listened and didn't like it.

'It just doesn't sound like me,' he said.

I found that difficult. *No More Shall We Part* was the end of us working together and it felt like Nick wasn't as open to suggestions. Once he cleaned up he could do everything himself. He knew what he wanted and had learnt the recording process. In fact, he probably understood it much earlier but couldn't be bothered. Instead, he'd point the boat in the right direction and leave it to someone else. It's bittersweet because I'd love to still work with him, but I wouldn't have the energy to keep up anyway.

I was at the band's video shoot for 'Fifteen Feet of Pure White Snow'. Noah Taylor was there, Jarvis Cocker, Jason Donovan. Jason was having a good day, he was heavily affected. We were told to dress in 1970s clothes and dance badly, which was easy. I was there all day dancing like an idiot in a brown, ill-fitting suit. I must have been really bad because when the clip came out I'd got cut. How disappointing. That makes it a fourth time, doesn't it?

T.C.

Moving to England was a mistake. I thought there'd be work but I was wrong. There was none and the business had started dropping off everywhere. It was tough. We were living in commission flats and Astrid was bringing in the money teaching while I sat at home with drug dealers outside the door.

Their music went all day. *DOOF-DOOF-DOOF-DOOF!*

I couldn't stand it anymore and had to get home. I returned to Australia in 2001 and to my surprise the situation was the same. Record companies were only dealing with the biggest names and the biggest studios. All the good work was going to a handful of people, and I wasn't one of them.

Long Gone Whistle

(2002)

Pro Tools is a computer program used for recording which began to appear in studios in the mid-1990s, replacing tape machines and ADATs. I wasn't very impressed with the early versions, but as it improved I realised it was here to stay.

But I didn't adjust to the change well.

I can use Pro Tools but am so bloody slow it's not worth it. I move the mouse and click here, there and everywhere. It blows the momentum of the session. But that's just me – there are plenty of people who are really good at it, like Chris Thompson. He'd set up Martin Street, a small recording studio in Brighton. I was living in the drum booth.

Chris would get cross as he attempted to teach me.

'Look, Tony,' he'd say. 'It's really easy. This is what you do!'

I just stood staring cross-eyed at the computer screen. I didn't understand. I'm sure I could have, but I didn't feel the need. I was starting to lose interest.

T.C.

I've got a lot of respect for my brother, he's a smart man. Martin learnt his trade studying cane toads and how to get rid of them. We've had some of the best times together. He'd take me out into the bush and point out things city folk don't know.

'See that ripple in the lake?' he'd say. 'Keep an eye on it.'

Next thing, a platypus would appear.

In 2002 Astrid and I moved to the small town of Warburton. It seemed like a good idea at the time, I wasn't in great health or brimming with enthusiasm. Diabetes was stopping me from doing what I had always loved. I tried to record Dark Horses' *Sweet Nothing* with Tex Perkins and Charlie Owen at Festival Studios the following year but it was a lottery, I couldn't promise a full day's work. I went from being really fussy with mixes, to whacking them down quickly. Maybe it was because I'd had so much practice? Or maybe it was bending over the console to reach the equalisers. I like to spend quite a bit of time making adjustments and my back would begin to hurt. I don't think it's a bad back, more like a bad liver.

Tex's *The Man in Black* Johnny Cash tour a few years later took me by surprise. It was a good business move, but not who I remembered him to be. Tex is an observant person and always learning. You can almost see his mind ticking over, sifting through what he thinks is useful and what is not, which is why he goes from strength to strength.

T.C.

Underland was a dance piece by American choreographer Stephen Petronio set to the music of Nick Cave, commissioned by the Sydney Dance Company in 2003. I didn't have a clue what to do and was only there because Nick couldn't get involved.

I got some of the original 2-inch multitrack tapes and stripped the song arrangements back. It was great fun to revisit those old recordings, but such a kerfuffle to access the tapes that in the end I didn't do much. A soundscape artist came along and inserted weird effects to link each song. I didn't really understand what he was doing, but everyone was happy.

The choreographer, Stephen, was a character.

We had a photo taken together in a grubby alleyway for *The Age* newspaper. It's bloody funny. He's standing there with a shaved bald head, looking as camp as a row of pink tents, next to my dirty, half-dreadlocked hair. What a queer couple.

Stephen stayed for the premiere then went back to America. I remember complaining to him bitterly that Nick's music wasn't loud enough. The sound of the dancers' feet hitting the stage was louder than the music! But of course that's the way it had to be. He was catering to a completely different audience from those who had recorded the music. Gough Whitlam and his wife were sitting in front of me in the audience. I wonder what Gough made of Nick Cave's music? He appeared to be quite enjoying it.

Dance is a mystery to me, so too opera. I don't understand what people like about it, but those who do love it with a passion. So be it. I am passionate about the music I like. The after-party was an education and a side of arty life I'd never seen before, awash with expensive free booze.

'Oh darling, marvellous!'

T.C.

Not long ago I bought a copy of John Lennon's *Imagine* on CD. I put it on and thought, *Fuck! There's something wrong with this!* It sounded completely different to the album I love. I checked the cover and it said, *remixed by Yoko Ono*, so I took it back to the shop in disgust.

I don't like remixed records.

When you're happy with something, leave it. Remastering is totally different and these days it's very difficult to find an album that hasn't been 'Digitally Remastered'. It improves the sound, usually. The Bad Seeds began reissuing their catalogue and got me in to advise on new surround sound mixes. The engineer wanted to know how I'd got specific sounds but I couldn't remember, so I just told him to add a lot of treble EQ and some short reverb to the snare. Surround sound doesn't do much for me. I enjoy the effect when I'm watching films, but when listening to music I prefer two speakers in front of me. I suppose I'm a bit of a dinosaur.

The CD format was a necessary evil. Like the iPod and now streaming, I wasn't happy with the reduced sound quality, but it's better than nothing at all. You have to consider all these different formats and listening conditions when you're mixing. Most people hear music on car radios, earphones and crappy home stereos, not big studio speakers. For the general public, stereo often just means you can play the music in two different rooms. I remember going to people's houses and finding one speaker in the lounge room and the other in the kitchen!

Going mono helps. In the early days we always checked mixes in mono to see how it would sound on AM radio. You'd be horrified how much of an instrument was lost, so would turn that fader up a bit more. And that doesn't hurt.

T.C.

People say I can sing but I disagree, I can mimic and that's not singing. A good singer has something original, their own voice. Unfortunately there's more than a few mimics out there.

Talent shows started springing up on television: *Australian Idol, The X Factor, Australia's Got Talent*. They really annoyed me. I thought, *What the fuck? Do people really like this?* I expected more from music and got a little bitter. I had grown up in pioneering times when sounds were created on the spot. The things I saw engineers do at Armstrong's blew my mind — slashing speakers with razor blades to get distortion, manipulating tape machines for phasing effects. It was a challenge and the impromptu experimentation was half the fun.

That's what I miss about recording now. As it's become more computerised something has been lost. You no longer find a great-sounding room but instead build it in a virtual space.

On a screen.

Computers were supposed to save time, but they waste time instead. There's too many options! I'm not saying it's wrong, it's just not the way I learnt. To all the young dudes recording that way, good luck for understanding it, because I don't. But I'm a lazy bastard. I find playing with a computer hard work and think it's much easier to walk around and use your ears. 'Hey, check out this stairwell. I bet that will sound great!' Nine times out of ten it did.

T.C.

For a while living in Warburton was good. I took up woodcarving. Eventually, though, there wasn't much to do except drink. I wanted to get back into the studio and show young bastards how recording works.

Unfortunately we didn't have Armstrong's anymore.

Ernie Rose kept the studio going under the Metropolis name for as long as he could, but closed it in 2006. Studio 3, the mixing room, was the last to go. All that remained of the studio was Ernie's mobile recording truck. Fortunately, Atlantis had relocated to Port Melbourne and Dave McCluney had a 2-inch 24-track tape machine that he maintained nicely, so the studio was analogue and digital. It was great – I'd ask him to do something on Pro Tools, go off for a cigarette, come back and it was done.

I loved working with Dave. He's an organised, what-you-see-is-what-you-get sort of person, but as an engineer he did some wacky things. He would build his own gizmos, none of which had covers, so there'd be valves and live wires exposed. Dave was the only person who could operate them! God bless him, he struggled through shit. He's patient and will sit for hours while artists work things out, which I was for a while too. I hear funny stories about Dave. People say he bends over the desk, fiddles with a couple of knobs, then leaps back to listen, exactly as I would. They say imitation is the sincerest form of flattery. That is one of the nicest compliments I could get.

T.C.

A couple of years ago I had an unpleasant experience working on an album for a young band from Sydney. They had tickets on themselves and a manager who was licking their boots. They were going to be the next big thing.

No they weren't, they were shit.

Musicians play the music and I try to make it sound good. That's the way it's always been for me. The guitarist in the band was lovely, but he hadn't thought about what he was doing. He recorded twenty guitar tracks for each song, just because he could. It's a problem created by Pro Tools – you leave decisions until later. Not to be outdone, the singer recorded sixteen lead vocal tracks and didn't just edit words together, but syllables. That's no way to create music!

We went to Sing Sing Studios in Richmond to mix and it was horrible. The singer and the guitarist didn't get along, so the two of them would fight and carry on. I got fed up and turned all twenty guitar tracks on at once.

'What does that sound like?' I said. 'It sounds like shit. A blur.'

'Well,' came their reply, 'it's up to you to sort it out.'

I didn't like that idea, so they got someone else to mix it. I couldn't be bothered listening to twenty guitar tracks, let alone choose. It's sad because that experience put me off recording and I haven't wanted to work since.

T.C.

The last album I produced and engineered was Charlie Owen's *Turn the Light On* at Atlantis in 2009. It's all soundscapes. Way-out stuff, not at all what you'd expect from him. Charlie didn't care, he just wanted to do what he wanted to do.

Like all good artists he had a vision.

Maurice Frawley died in May and it was one of the saddest losses. I worked with Charlie the following year on a tribute album, *Long Gone Whistle*, and recorded a few tracks with Don Walker, Paul Kelly and Tex Perkins. Divinyls' Chrissy Amphlett sang on one – it was the last time I saw her. She had a great attitude, even though she was obviously suffering. Those are the last sessions I did, quite a while ago now.

LISTEN
'Harness Down'
—Maurice Frawley and Working Class Ringos

You've got to be passionate about this job. You've really got to love it, otherwise you shouldn't be doing it. I knew something was wrong when I started arriving at the studio two or three hours late. I couldn't get out of bed and then would try to catch every red traffic light on the way.

T.C.

I haven't seen anyone for a while. I've become a bit of a recluse, which is not healthy. It's not good for your brain. We all need stimulation. 'If you don't use it, you lose it,' as my doctor likes to tell me. He's always right.

I would love to do more recording. Friends suggest projects but I don't feel comfortable getting in touch with artists and offering to work. I'd have to charge them money and musicians don't have any, particularly the ones I like. They seem to be the most broke of all! It saddens me that the music business has ended up that way and it's why so many artists record at home. These days you can fit a whole studio into the back of a car. Sometimes people contact me about it.

'I've done a recording on Pro Tools, can you mix it into an album?' they ask.

I could, but it's not something that gets me excited. I'd like to get together with a good band and record and mix the whole album. It's important. I know how I like to mic things up, and to find rooms that sound good. Besides, I'm not that old. At least before I'm sixty I should be able to finish a few things. Maybe even sixty-five? I hope so, but it depends what my doctor has to say. Lately my health has got pretty poor. It frustrates me, but I'm not giving up. I've had tests to find out why I'm feeling so sluggish.

T.C.

There's longevity in Mum's side of the family. My grandfather lived to his eighties, my grandmother her nineties, and an auntie made it to ninety. The Cohens, not so much. Dad's mother died reasonably young and his father in his seventies, but Dad is still kicking!

It reminds me how many people I've lost over the years.

Quite a few have fallen off the perch. I'm surprised to have outlived some, but I guess it's just the luck of the draw – when your cards come up, your cards come up. I get very upset when I lose another but I dream a lot. It's always a jumble of those who are with us and those who have gone, and I wake up happy because I feel like I've been in touch with them again.

Tony Cohen died on Wednesday, 2 August 2017. His final recording was for the Augie March Bootikins *album in May.*

LISTEN
'The Third Drink'—Augie March

A Note on the Text

Tony commenced work on his memoir in July 2012 with a note: *This will not be easy ... dates will have to be sorted out later after much research.* Following an oral history interview for the National Film and Sound Archive of Australia in 2013, he requested I assist him and this collaboration continued until his death in 2017. I interviewed Tony and his colleagues from May 2013 to July 2016 and the manuscript has been completed as envisaged, in Tony's own voice. Additional source material includes the following: Interview with Richard Cluff, *Sunglasses after Dark*, no. 2, 1986; Ian Johnston, *Bad Seed: The Biography of Nick Cave*, Little Brown, 1995; Interview with Mike Gribble, *The Advertiser*, 1995; Interview with Richard Kingsmill, ABC, 1995; Interview with Greg Simmons, *Sound Australasia*, vol. 1, issue 2, 1996; Clinton Walker, *Stranded: The Secret History of Australian Independent Music 1977–1991*, Pan Macmillan, 1996; Interview, *Long Way to the Top*, ABC, 2001; Interview, *Conversations with Richard Fidler*, ABC, 2006; Dale Blair, *Life in a Padded Cell: A Biography of Tony Cohen*, 2016.

John Olson, 2023

In Memoriam

(listed in order of appearance)

Hubert Mackinolty (1897–1979)

Phillip Cohen (1927–2016)

Peter Hatwell (1955–1983)

John Ahern (1957–2018)

Lawrence Costin (1933–2007)

John Sayers (1945–2020)

Billy Thorpe (1946–2007)

Teddy Toi (1940–2022)

Jack Richardson (1929–2011)

Graham Thirkell (1937–2010)

Duncan McGuire (1943–1989)

Jim Keays (1946–2014)

Lobby Loyde (1941–2007)

Stevie Dunstan (b. 1942)

Smacka Fitzgibbon (1930–1979)

Ron Tudor (1924–2020)

K.D. Firth (1945–2018)

Ian Mawson (1938–2008)

Ian Davis (1952–1989)

Michael Gudinski (1952–2021)

Grant McLennan (1958–2006)

Buster Stiggs (1954–2018)

Stephan Fidock (1959–2020)

Doug Parkinson (1946–2021)

Steve Prestwich (1954–2011)

Spencer P. Jones (1956–2018)

Chris Bailey (1956–2022)

Ian Rilen (1947–2006)

Bob Nimmo (1955–1986)

Michael Hutchence (1960–1997)

John Murphy (1959–2015)

Epic Soundtracks (1959–1997)

Nikki Sudden (1956–2006)

Jeffrey Lee Pierce (1958–1996)

Roland Wolf (1965–1995)

Anita Lane (1960–2021)

Mick Geyer (1953–2004)

Bruno Adams (1963–2009)

Brian Hooper (1962–2018)

Tony Pola (1961–2021)

Nicky Hopkins (1944–1994)

Bobby Keys (1943–2014)

Peter Lillie (1951–2012)

Rowland S. Howard (1959–2009)

Tracy Pew (1957–1986)

James Freud (1959–2010)

Ben Wallace-Crabbe (1959–1986)

Johnny Crash (d. 2014)

James Cruickshank (1962–2015)

Speedy (d. 1996)

Maurice Frawley (1954–2009)

Shane Walsh (1959–2011)

Ross Hannaford (1950–2016)

Wayne Duncan (1944–2016)

Conway Savage (1960–2018)

Chrissy Amphlett (1959–2013)

Select Discography

(listed in order of recording date)
P=producer, E=engineer, M=mixer, A=assistant

1974

BILLY THORPE AND THE AZTECS, *More Arse than Class*   A

MISS LINDA GEORGE, *Linda*   A

JIM KEAYS, *The Boy from the Stars*   E

1975

CHAD MORGAN, *One of the Mob*   E

PAUL MCKAY SOUND,

'Take You Where the Music's Playing' (single)   E, M

1976

SUPERNAUT, *Supernaut*   P, E, M

LOBBY LOYDE, *Beyond Morgia: The Labyrinths of Klimster*   E, M

1977

THE FERRETS, *Dreams of a Love*   E, M

VARIOUS, *Nightmovin' Live*   M

1978

THE FERRETS, *Fame at Any Price*	P, E, M
MARK GILLESPIE & THE VICTIMS, *The Black Tape*	E, M
CLINT SMALL, *Crack in the Wall* (EP)	P, E, M

1979

THE BOYS NEXT DOOR, *Door, Door*	E, M
MONDO ROCK, *Primal Park*	E
THE BOYS NEXT DOOR, *Hee Haw* (EP)	E, M
SPLIT ENZ, 'Things' (single)	P, E, M

1980

JAMES FREUD, *Breaking Silence*	E, M
LAUGHING CLOWNS, *Laughing Clowns* (EP)	E, M
THE BOYS NEXT DOOR, *The Birthday Party*	E, M
LAUGHING CLOWNS, *Sometimes, The Fire Dance....* (EP)	E, M
MODELS, *Alphabravocharliedeltaechofoxtrotgolf*	E, M
MAGAZINE, *Play*	E
THE REELS, *Five Great Gift Ideas*	E, M
THE DOTS, *The Dots* (EP)	E, M

1981

THE BIRTHDAY PARTY, *Prayers on Fire*	E, M
THE EARS, 'Scarecrow' (single)	E, M
MODELS, *Cut Lunch* (EP)	P, E, M
SERIOUS YOUNG INSECTS, 'Trouble Understanding Words' (single)	E, M
THE GO-BETWEENS, *Send Me a Lullaby*	P, E, M
HUNTERS & COLLECTORS, *World of Stone* (EP)	P, E, M
HUNTERS & COLLECTORS, *Hunters & Collectors*	E

1982

THE BIRTHDAY PARTY, *Junkyard*	E, M
THE GO-BETWEENS, 'Hammer the Hammer' (single)	P, E, M
PEL MEL, *Out of Reason*	P, E, M
THE REELS, *Pitt Street Farmers* (EP)	P
MODELS, demo	E, M
SACRED COWBOYS, 'Nothing Grows in Texas' (single)	E, M

1983

PEL MEL, *Persuasion*	P, E, M
COLD CHISEL, *Twentieth Century*	E, M
BEASTS OF BOURBON, *The Axeman's Jazz*	E, M

1984

THE SAINTS, *A Little Madness to Be Free*	E, M
DYNAMIC HEPNOTICS, 'Soul Kind of Feeling' (single)	E
THE JOHNNYS, *The Johnnys* (EP)	E, M
PAUL KELLY, demo	E, M
THE JOHNNYS, *Highlights of a Dangerous Life*	E

1985

X, *At Home with You*	E

1986

NICK CAVE & THE BAD SEEDS, *Kicking against the Pricks*	E
MICHAEL HUTCHENCE, 'Rooms for the Memory' (single)	E
NICK CAVE & THE BAD SEEDS, *Your Funeral… My Trial*	P, E, M

1987

THESE IMMORTAL SOULS, *Get Lost (Don't Lie)*	E, M
THE GUN CLUB, demo	E, M
CRIME & THE CITY SOLUTION, *Shine*	E, M

1988

NICK CAVE & THE BAD SEEDS, *Tender Prey* — E, M
THE BUTCHER SHOP, *Hard For You* (EP) — E, M

1989

THE GO-BETWEENS, demo — E, M

1990

GRANT MCLENNAN, *Watershed* — E

1991

THE CRUEL SEA, *This Is Not the Way Home* — P, E, M
BEASTS OF BOURBON, *The Low Road* — P, E, M

1992

NICK CAVE & THE BAD SEEDS, *Henry's Dream* — E, M
MIXED RELATIONS, *Take It or Leave It* (EP) — P, M
STRAITJACKET FITS, *Done* (EP) — P, E, M
KIM SALMON & THE SURREALISTS, *Sin Factory* — P, E, M
TEX, DON & CHARLIE, *Sad but True* — E, M
DAVE GRANEY 'N' THE CORAL SNAKES,
Night of the Wolverine — P, E, M

1993

ANITA LANE, *Dirty Pearl* — E, M
NICK CAVE & THE BAD SEEDS, *Live Seeds* — E, M
THE CRUEL SEA, *The Honeymoon Is Over* — P, E, M
TIDDAS, *Sing about Life* — P, E, M
WILD PUMPKINS AT MIDNIGHT, *Going Sick* (EP) — P, E, M
NICK CAVE & THE BAD SEEDS, *Let Love In* — P, E, M

1994

PAUL KELLY, *Wanted Man* — E, M

POWDERFINGER, *Parables for Wooden Ears* — P, E, M

MAURICE FRAWLEY, *Livin' Lazy* — P, E, M

KIM SALMON & THE SURREALISTS,
Kim Salmon & the Surrealists — P, E, M

THE CRUEL SEA, *Three Legged Dog* — P, E, M

1995

MICK HARVEY, *Intoxicated Man* — P, E

NICK CAVE & THE BAD SEEDS, *Murder Ballads* — P, E, M

THE BLACKEYED SUSANS, *Mouth to Mouth* — P, M

DIRTY THREE, demo — E

BEASTS OF BOURBON, *Gone* — E, M

1997

ASTRID MUNDAY, *Astrid Munday* — P, E, M

VARIOUS, *Recovery (Hits from the Back Door)* — P

1998

LODGER, *Walk in the Park* — M

COLD CHISEL, *The Last Wave of Summer* — E, M

2000

NICK CAVE & THE BAD SEEDS, *No More Shall We Part* — P, E, M

2009

CHARLIE OWEN, *Turn the Light On* — P, E, M

VARIOUS, *Long Gone Whistle, The Songs Of Maurice Frawley* — P, E, M

2017

AUGIE MARCH, *Bootikins* — E, M

Acknowledgements

John would like to thank the following, in alphabetical order, for their assistance and/or support: Ken Berryman, Nick Cave, Margaret Cohen, Martin Cohen, Katie Dixon, Patrick Donovan, Chris Feik, Mick Harvey, Andrew Hehir, Jeff Jenkins, Peter Lunt, Molly Meldrum, Billy Miller, Kate Morgan, Astrid Munday, John Nolan, Allen Olson, Patricia Olson, Melanie Ostell, Charlie Owen, Martin Sleeman, Callum Smith, Chris Thompson and Don Walker.